Clark Gordon

Shylock;

As Banker, Bondholder, Corruptionist, Conspirator

Clark Gordon

Shylock;
As Banker, Bondholder, Corruptionist, Conspirator

ISBN/EAN: 9783337818036

Hergestellt in Europa, USA, Kanada, Australien, Japan

Cover: Foto ©ninafisch / pixelio.de

Weitere Bücher finden Sie auf **www.hansebooks.com**

AS

BANKER,
BONDHOLDER,
CORRUPTIONIST,
CONSPIRATOR.

BY

Gordon Clark.

Author of "Man's Birthright" (Putnam's Sons); "The People's Right in Wealth" (North American Review); "Scientific Taxation". (North American Review), etc.

AUTHOR'S PUBLISHER,

c/o *the American Bimetallic League, Sun Building, Washington, D. C.*

1894.

COPYRIGHT, 1894, BY M. D. CLARK.

PUBLISHER'S NOTE.

The author of this book desires its readers to know that he alone is responsible for the special monetary opinions expressed in it, and for its plain criticism of public men. No party, and no organization, may precisely coincide with him in all respects. But his views on the demonetization of silver, as the greatest crime of modern times, being generally entertained by those who understand the subject, the AMERICAN BIMETALLIC LEAGUE has kindly arranged to aid the publisher in placing the whole truth of that matter before the people.

DEDICATION.

In memory of a revered personal friend, my first instructor
as well in the lessons of
MONEY,
a question which he considered next in immediate practical importance
to the
ABOLITION OF SLAVERY;
in sacred memory, once more, of his aggressive manner
of treating
THE PUBLIC ENEMIES OF HIS COUNTRY;
I dedicate this tract-militant to the inspiring soul and the
mighty work of the grandest American
I ever knew—

WENDELL PHILLIPS.

Were he alive, my native State of
MASSACHUSETTS,
with the rest of New England, would not now be the most ignorant
section of North America on the most
vital subject of the age,
EXCEPTING ONLY NEW YORK
—for many years my home—the great Empire State of
MONOPOLY, PLUTOCRACY,
and their purchased implement of economic darkness called
AN "INDEPENDENT PRESS."
But knowing, as Wendell Phillips knew, that the patient masses,
"THE PLAIN PEOPLE,"
of New York and New England, as well as of the
WEST AND SOUTH,
are sound at heart, having only
FALLEN AMONG KNAVES,
I have perfect faith in the ultimate enlightenment and salvation of my
distracted country. My friends, read, THINK, VOTE! And,
at any cost, let us preserve the welfare
of mankind in this Republic!

PREFACE.

This bit of work is

FIRST: A plain, simple treatment of the Principles of Money, explained chiefly through the facts of history.

SECOND: An indictment of the English Banking-System, root and branch, which is now the worst confidence-game that cheats and curses the world.

THIRD: An unhesitating exposure of the corrupt Monetary-Legislation of the United States during and since the Civil War—a matter which the people have never understood, and which they can never sufficiently resent.

FOURTH: A terse, truthful account of the Demonetization of Silver, the motives which led to it, and the malefactors who participated in that most criminal conspiracy of the modern world.

FIFTH: An appeal to the people to rouse themselves for the abolition of A New Form of Slavery, which European aristocrats and American Tories are plotting to impose on this country—the slavery of pauper-serfs as absolute dependents on a worse than "baronial" Money-Power.

SIXTH: A call to American voters to save THEMSELVES, at the expense of any political party, or any set of public men, used as traitors to their country and enemies of mankind.

CONTENTS.

INTRODUCTION.	1
CHAPTER I: WHAT IS MONEY?	13
" II: GOLD AND SILVER AS MONEY.	14
" III: THE FIRST GREAT BANK.	15
" IV: SHYLOCK'S BANK OF ENGLAND.	17
" V: OUR COLONIAL MONEY.	21
" VI: THE ENGLISH SPAWN, OUR OLD STATE BANKS.	26
" VII: THE SHYLOCK "PATRIOTS" OF 1861.	29
" VIII: SHYLOCK'S DEFEAT OF HONEST MONEY.	33
" IX: THE "NATIONAL" PROGENY OF THE "STATE" BANKS.	43
" X: HUGH MCCULLOCH'S DAY OF TRAMPS.	46
" XI: "SPECIE-RESUMPTION."	53
" XII: SHYLOCK'S MASTERPIECE, THE CRIME OF 1873.	55
" XIII: EFFECTS OF THE CRIME OF 1873.	102
" XIV: THE REMEDY.	116

INTRODUCTION.

Soon after the first inauguration of Abraham Lincoln as President of the United States, he was met, one morning, by an old acquaintance, a banker, who happened to be in Washington. "Mr. President," said he, "how are you going to raise funds to carry on the war?" "It must be done," replied Mr. Lincoln, "but I don't know *how*: I don't know anything about money, and, to tell the truth, I never had much respect for anybody who did." Our great and good President had no time and no heart, just then, to consider the banker's question, and, quite as he said, he had never informed himself in the principles of money. It was a great pity. For had he been familiar with those principles, we may be sure that he would have insisted on saving the productive toilers of his country about one half of their interest-bearing war-debt, which, in 1865, amounted to some twenty-four hundred millions of dollars.* Putting the figures at the lowest point of such experts as have dared to be honest in their statements, a thousand millions, with the interest added, might possibly reach the part of that debt which the money-class, as such, filched from the rest of us--soldiers, workers, widows and orphans.† Those greedy and remorseless "sharks" did not exactly *steal* this vast property belonging to their fellow-citizens: they only wheedled and coerced a few of our public servants to procure the passage of certain laws for them, by which they could commit virtual larceny without going to jail. So they were not "thieves." They were "highly respectable gentlemen," as the world now goes, because their "manipulations" were large; but, compared with their *legalized crimes,* the technical and punishable crimes against property of all other classes of our people, from that day to this, have been like the moral lapses of infants at the breast.

THOSE MONSTROUS SHYLOCKS, however, were *successful,* and they lived unwhipped of justice. Emboldened by this result, the same band—partly the old generation and partly new recruits of two continents—have since combined, with their headquarters in England, to despoil, for what they can make out of it, the honest, industrious, common people of *the whole world.* This is the short of that much more than tragic affair, commonly dubbed "*the demonetization of silver.*"

We have all heard that silver is "the money of the poor." So it is, in nearly every country on earth. It has no fixed, "intrinsic" value.

---

* The *whole* public debt stood at $2,844,649,000.

† In this book, every statement of vital importance is explained, with the facts, figures and authorities, in the proper historical order.

Neither has gold.* "Intrinsic value" is always the chatter of a dunce, when it is not the shout of a rascal. If both gold and silver were suddenly and everywhere disused as money, one would not, for the time, be much more valuable than the other, as the demand for neither would be at all equal to the supply. The value of both consists, not to say largely, but chiefly, in the fact that they have been coined for centuries into *money*, *regulated by law*, and have thus been invested with a *money-demand*.

Again, it is perfectly well known, whoever may be procured to deny it, that all the gold and all the silver in existence would not, if coined in present specie, amount to a fifth of the ready cash required for trade. Taking fully into mind every bank and clearing-house of the modern world, with their checks, drafts, and bills of exchange, there is needed, in addition, many times the amount of all the "precious metals" afloat, if business is ever to be done *without dishonest inflations of credit*, and without *perpetually recurring panics*.† THE CLAIM THAT "THERE IS MONEY ENOUGH" always comes from those who want to monopolize it, want to inflate and contract it—want to cheat with it. But no: the claim, or at least the echo of it, does sometimes come from the dupes and victims of some bank, who talk as they are bidden when they ask for loans.

THE WORLD'S STOCK OF GOLD-COIN TO-DAY is about thirty-six hundred millions, and the accumulated stock of SILVER COIN, about four thousand millions.‡ This makes in all seventy-six hundred millions, or say, in round numbers, *six dollars a head* for the world's population of twelve hundred million souls. If silver could actually be taken out of monetary use, we—mankind as a whole—would have left, in gold, the magnificent allowance of three dollars each, with which to conduct our affairs. But, as the gold is everywhere locked up in public treasuries, war-chests and bank-vaults, for "reserves," we should not have even that. We could not possibly have anything but some inflation of it—some indefinite multiplication, in the form of bank-paper, or debased token money. This swindling stuff is what Jew-bankers and their Gentile confederates, in Europe and America, are perpetually screaming about as "an honest dollar." It is the dollar of malefactors, pure and simple; only they buy laws to uphold villainy. Still, we are obliged to take the credit-bubbles, the big inflations of their little gold-pot, in exchange for our labor, our manufactures, our produce and our estates. That is to say, WE MUST HAVE

---

* This has been settled too long for patient argument. "Intrinsic value" has been a corpse—not only dead but buried—ever since Adam Smith wrote his "Wealth of Nations," and said: "Gold and silver, like every other commodity, vary in their value. The quantity of labor which any particular quantity of these can purchase or command, or the quantity of goods it will exchange for, depends always on the fertility or barrenness of the mines which happen to be known about the time when such exchanges are made. * * * A commodity which is itself continually varying in its own value, can never be an accurate measure of the value of other commodities."—Book I., Chapter 5.

† For a specific illustration, see last chapter.

‡ The figures of the U. S. Mint.

MONEY TO DO BUSINESS. But when the inflation of the gold-pot is rounded out to the right size, those who *blew* it always *burst* it. They "*call in their gold.*" Then, at once, every moneyed institution is obliged to cut down its loans, or become insolvent. The scoundrel's one gold dollar will not pay the five, or ten, or twenty dollars, which it promises to "redeem." THE PROMISE IS A FRAUD; but, by means of this fraud, the jugglers of gold command our very bread and shelter at Shylock's price. His price we know. It is the property itself, more or less, or as much as he dares to take without losing his own by revolution. The sheriff takes our possessions for him, while we become paupers and tramps, and either end life or begin it anew.

Such is the national and international game of those pirates of our present civilization to whom has recently been given the name of "gold-bugs." But the game is not new. The leaders of it have deliberately planned and remorselessly carried it out, at brief intervals, in various countries, for the past hundred and fifty years. But *now*, they have enlarged their plans to the size of the earth. They have absorbed politicians, editors, economists, and so-called "statesmen"—all the public mercenaries that can be had for hire or place in every nation—and have put their agents, attorneys and lackeys in every large centre of industry. They mean to *corner us completely*—to set their own measure of value on everything that is raised, made or sold, and thus to dictate the material condition of the human race. But they are cold and calculating. They take one step at a time. Owning the bonded-debts of the nations, payable in gold, the first step is to make the gold scarce and dear. Controlling the supply of it themselves, they can double the demand at will, increasing their principal and interest at the expense of every tax-payer and producer in every land, for *every land is in debt to them.* In this way their universal monopoly takes our first " pound of flesh," and the blood that goes with it.

BUT "THE SILVER-MEN"—what about *them?* Well, in the present issue—the great battle for honest money—the silver-men, if by that term we mean the silver-*producers*, are so small a factor that they would be almost of no consequence, if they had not been robbed and outraged. The silver-producers of our country have some seventy-five millions of dollars a year at stake in their product. But the wheat-producers, the corn-producers, the cotton-producers—these three classes of American producers alone—lose annually about *a thousand millions* through the gold-plot against the silver dollar.* It is a plot against every legitimate business known to man. The silver-*miners*, in struggling for their own interests, have been obliged to become the people's champions and defenders. But the silver-*men*, in the large sense, are the PEOPLE THEMSELVES, who demand an honest volume of metallic money, according to the custom of all ages and the Constitution of the United States.

* This statement, which is in no way exaggerated, will be explained in detail as we proceed.

From the beginning of history, gold and silver have been used to stand for the value of other things. At first, in primeval Asia, the relation of value between the two metals depended simply on the proportion in which they were found. The most general relation of ancient times appears to have been as one ounce of gold to twelve ounces of silver.* But the modern world, at the outset of its vast increase of production and commercial exchange, placed silver at the ratio of between fifteen and sixteen to one, and so established it in the coinage of nations. The silver has been passed out by law, and has gone into the hands of the people for generations. The people, certainly, have had none too much of it, at the full value of its issue to them. To decrease its purchasing power, its debt-paying power, is to cheat the people out of whatever difference may result from the scheme. But the cheat was begun, by aid of the government of England, in the year 1816. For an *individual*, to counterfeit or debase a coin of England, is to commit a crime, to incur disgrace, and to merit a cell in prison. But, for the British Parliament to counterfeit all value, by debasing the shilling of every British subject, is to sit with "honor," and enact a law, at the beck of men like the first Baron Rothschild, who could absorb the indebtedness of nations by serenely speculating over the carnage of Waterloo. For such men, silver was demonetized, that one of the money-metals might be got out of the way, and the other made scarcer, dearer, and more easily monopolized. The English demonetizer, Lord Liverpool, said that, as nations increase in wealth, their money should increase in value.† The Gentile was a good Jew; but, at that time, his "gentle blood" could speak for Jerusalem better than Jerusalem could speak for itself.

In 1848 gold was discovered in California, and at about the same time in Australia. This new wealth filled the whole family of Shylock with horror. As gold increased in quantity, they feared it would de-crease in the power of buying and controlling other things. They had enjoyed the advantage of its *scarcity* for thousands of years; but now the bread and meat of the people stood for a fifth more of "the precious metals" than when mankind were going about half-fed and half-clothed.‡ So Shylock *declared war on* GOLD, and filled the heads of writers, economists and journalists with his sorrows. De Quincey ate a little opium, and dreamed for the public that gold would soon have no value at all—would be as intrinsic mud and stones. But Chevalier took the matter profoundly to heart, and wrote a series of papers, in 1854-5 and 6, which were collected

*On authority of the coin-experts, like Max Müller.
†"The Silver Question," by Geo. M. Weston, Secretary of the U. S. Monetary Commission, page 27.
‡Exactly how great the effect was [of Australian and Californian gold] may not be agreed, but the accepted statement is that it was an augmentation of one-fifth in general prices during rather less than half the term of one generation.—"The Silver Question": Weston, page 2.

in a book called "The Fall of Gold"—translated into English by Cobden. The gist of Chevalier was that gold was becoming so plenty that its value must decline, and that Europe must guard against it without delay.* The knights of the money-bag massed their forces: Holland had already demonetized gold—as early as 1847. Belgium followed in 1850, and Germany, with Austria, in 1857. THEY ALL WENT TO "THE SILVER BASIS." But England had committed herself too far the other way, and her sly agents, sent out to California and Australia, reported that the new "goldfields" were more limited than the "silver-beds." Then the Continental money-lenders, with Chevalier as their fugleman, faced about, retraced their steps, and joined hands with their brotherhood in England.†

It was not difficult to demonetize silver in Europe. The people of the United States are supposed to have established a government devoted to their own welfare—a government "of the people, by the people, and for the people." The governments of Europe are governments of aristocrats, by aristocrats, and for aristocrats. The classes make the laws, or remake

---

* In the light of this one fact alone, think of the pure brass of any *intelligent* person who pretends to find "intrinsic value" in a piece of yellow metal.

† The facts of this historical summary are perfectly familiar to everybody who really knows anything about the money-question. They have been repeated, over and over again, in the Congress of the United States. For instance, in 1878, Senator D. W. Voorhees, who in 1893 accepted the position of first-trombone in John Sherman's financial orchestra, played his instrument thus:

"It was in the interest of this powerful class [the money-lenders] that silver was demonetized in 1873, not because it was not less valuable as money than gold, but simply because retired capital desired to diminish the amount of money of every kind circulating in the hands of the people. The managers of the great money centers in this country and in Europe saw with avaricious alarm the bright streams of silver beginning to increase in volume and in value * * * and now we hear from their angry throats and from an apparently still angrier newspaper press *which they control*, a cry without ceasing against silver-inflation arising from an overproduction of the metal. They have heretofore filled the world with their hostile clamor mainly against a paper currency not immediately convertible into coin of intrinsic value; but it now appears that there can be, in their own amiable language, an insane inflation of a currency which has this very intrinsic value in itself. We now perceive that even these precious metals may become more abundant than is agreeable to those who *want the purchasing power of money increased by lessening the quantity in circulation, until $50 will buy in a farm worth a thousand, under the foreclosure of a mortgage*. * * * When the revelation of gold took place in California and on the other side of the world in Australia about the same time, an impulse was given to the progress of mankind greater than had been produced by any other event since Columbus discovered America. The whole world rejoiced, with one exception. The creditor class in every clime beneath the sun looked on in sullen distrust and dread. * * * In 1856 * * this class broke forth in different countries in favor of *demonetizing gold*, because the supply was making money too plentiful. * * * Germany and Austria, and some other European governments, in 1857, actually *demonetized gold, in order to maintain the scarcity of money*. The reason why this question did not seriously agitate the financial circles of the United States is to be found in the fact that at that time we had no great creditor class in this country; we had no stupendous national debt held as an investment for fixed incomes; no such State, municipal and corporation debts as have since filled all the stock-markets with interest-bearing bonds, and which are now a draining tax on all the labor and production of the country."—*Congressional Record*, January 15th, 1878, page 334.

them, at will, and the masses live on the crumbs of such legislation. Two classes in Europe—the millionaire-bankers and the titled snobs—demonetized silver, by asking for a monetary revolution in their special interest, though Bismarck is said to have regretted Germany's concession to them, acknowledging, in his strong, frank way, that he was overreached by their machinations. In America, the case was different. However the attempt may now be made to cover it up, demonetization was procured by methods that would debauch panders and degrade pickpockets; and our subsequent silver-legislation, including the preposterously-named "Sherman law," has been a temporary and inadequate reaction against pure conspiracy and robbery.* The scheme was first projected in Europe, as long ago as 1867. In it were the lees and remnants of the old feudal aristocracy, the modern hook-nosed aristocrats of the gold-bond, and the leading confidence-men of the English bank-system, with a large Tory branch in America, represented even then by John Sherman. By this union of rich anarchists, England, in special, has found a new way to attack American institutions and the American people. By controlling the price of *our* silver, through *our* laws passed in *her* interest, she first makes enormous profits on the silver in India and the East, and then buys Indian products, *with that very silver*, so low as to shut American products out of the European markets. In this subtile way—which so many Americans have still too little sense to comprehend—England has reduced the price of American labor, crops and fabrics, *about one half* since 1873. What our *Tories* get out of the deal is the increasing value of every dollar for the rich-man which the poor-man owes him, and control by the National Banks of the people's volume of currency, so that money-lenders can inflate, contract and explode values, every five or ten years, and, by this thimble-rig, turn over the results of labor and skill to bullionists, misers, and usurers. This operation is what a London bank-man, named Hazard, bluntly described to American capitalists in 1862, as a means by which African slavery might be superseded—"*a new plan, led on by England,*" taking the place of the old system.† Truly. What is abject poverty and dependence for a people, white or black, but A FORM OF SLAVERY? It is practically slavery, with all its evils, but, as the same delectable Mr. Hazard also pointed out, it involves no care of the laborer, by the capitalist, *except the control of his wages.*

But shall England impose her plan of white slavery upon the people of the United States? Having twice beaten England by arms, shall she conquer us at last by gold and false-pretenses? Mr. Andrew Carnegie, a transplanted North-Briton who is now an American citizen, has recently

---

*See Chapter XII., devoted to this subject. It has been carefully prepared, with full reference to the facts, and will stand the test of time and history.

†This seemingly incredible assertion is literally true, and complete proofs of it are given in Chapter XII.

prophesied a blissful syndicate of nations, in which the American eagle and the British lion shall lovingly lie down, each in the other's bosom, and conduct their politics in the halo of that honeymoon. The ablest and most high-minded editor now in England, Mr. W. T. Stead, occasionally sings a sweet lullaby of the same sort. Evidently these amiable souls are not acquainted with the British gold-plot against the "plain people" of the United States, as Lincoln called those who did the working and the fighting when he was President. WAR with England—and not a financial war, but a conflict of powder and dynamite—would be more merciful, better, and cheaper in the end, than to permit the permanent infliction upon us of her present money-conspiracy. While that conspiracy lasts, *England is our deadly foe*—quite as much our enemy as she was in 1776 or in 1812; though now, as then, many friends of ours might be counted, even in a British Parliament. And that *Americans* are participants in the British attack on their country, makes no difference. So were the richest aristocrats and money-sharks, in the days of the Revolution. Those despicable "TORIES" were not more dangerous, then, to American liberty and prosperity, than the shareholders, tassels and attorneys of the English gold-pot are to-day. This, of course, does not mean that everybody, either in Europe or America, who favors a single gold-standard of money, is essentially and deliberately a villain. It means only that he is such, *if he understands the principles of economics as applied to currency*. Bank-men, perhaps, as a *class*, demand the gold-basis. Are they all dishonest and unpatriotic? Certainly not. But because a man can count a pile of coin or paper, or decide on discounting a neighbor's note, it is no sign he knows anything about the science of money. A grocer can sell a dozen eggs without comprehending biology, and a tape-merchant may get rich, yet never have heard of the reason for the length of his yard-stick. Many *bankers* have never thought of money, at all, beyond their routine methods of accumulating it, and have less knowledge of it, as cause and effect, than some coal-heavers. All such "financiers" are merely innocent sheep, following a few tough old bell-wethers. But *these*, for a long time, have been "wiser than serpents," more stealthy and more deadly.

There is no doubt, too, that some professional politicians may side with Shylock, and not have been paid for it with either a bribe or a place. As late as 1893, it seemed possible, for a time, that *even a President* might be so economically unlearned, or so portly with misinformation, as to mistake a raid of usurers for an economic reform. But that charitable illusion has passed away.*

* Whatever the precise fact may turn out to be, it now looks as if every President of the United States since Lincoln—though with some instances of misguidance rather than wrong-intent—has been pledged in advance to Wall Street, the National Banks, and the European money-octopus, and has taken his office by virtue of their contributions to his election-expenses. The case of Cleveland appears to be merely the culmination of the betrayal of the country, bringing the band of Judas fully to light.

THE AMERICAN PEOPLE MUST LEARN THE LESSON OF MONEY, or they are LOST! For every man, woman and child in the land—as indeed in the world—it is the most vital question of practical welfare that can now engage the human mind. And it is *not* difficult. Journalistic attorneys and ostensible teachers of political economy are often suborned to *pretend* difficulty, and do it in proportion to the fee received; for the poor wretches must eat and drink, and harlotry of the pen is in great demand.

MONEY is nothing but divisible value, put into something for the purpose of exchanging property. A dollar, if an honest one, is a deed to a certain definite amount of food, shelter, clothing, or whatever else a human being needs or desires. For easy illustration, dollars have been likened to carts, as both dollars and carts are vehicles of exchange. Carts are required to draw goods from a person who sells to a person who buys them. Dollars are likewise required to effect such exchanges. Now, if carts are at any time too numerous for the cartage required of them, not all the carts can get work enough to do, and the price of carts and cartage declines. If it ever happens that dollars become too numerous for the exchange of property—which has sometimes been the case with *unlimited* paper issues—such nominal dollars will not buy a true dollar's worth of other things. Then, money, as its philosophers say, "depreciates." If carts, on the other hand, are too few for the exchange of merchandise, carts and cartage "go up" in price; and if legal-tender dollars are too few for their work—a state of things that bankers and money-dealers are forever combining to effect—then money "*ap*-preciates," or every dollar of it commands an unjust, a dishonest value, in labor or flour, shoes or stockings. In short, the value of money—whether gold, silver, or legal-tender of any sort, depends, like everything else, on *the one basic law of all political economy, the law of supply and demand.*

Does so much cogitation split any head? If not, the head can take in the money-question well enough; for here is the bottom of it.

A book cannot be crowded into the "Introduction." But there is one thing in connection with our subject, against which Americans of to-day must be specially warned, and which they should treat with special contempt. As Britons, Germans-Jews, and Tories, have devised an economic conquest of the United States, Europe has sent over, from time to time, a lot of her literary barristers, Hessians and doctrinaires, or their works, and their apostles here have made much of these importations, as "great authorities." How much have we heard of Chevalier, Jevons, Victor Bonnet, Giffen, Cernuschi, with the rest of them, good, bad, and indifferent! Chevalier we have touched. Whatever else he may have done, he went nearly crazy for fear that the world's great specie-grabbers and credit-loaners would end their days in the poorhouse. He set up a shout for the demonetization of *gold*—a shout which he changed for the demonetization of *silver*. He had little influence in his own country. None of his fears have been realized, or his predictions fulfilled.* Bonnet was mostly an echo of Chevalier, and Giffen is an echo of the Bank of England. Jevons had the energy and industry of an English professor. Some of his facts are doubtless worth preserving, and not all of his theories are yet extinct. But he taught, for one thing, that silver could be disused as money in Europe and America, because "Asia is the reservoir and sink of the precious metals," taking "off our hands many millions of bullion which would be worse than useless." But, in such teachings, Jevons founded himself strictly on the span of his day—nothing beyond or better. That any possible amount of bullion in Britain, or anywhere else, can be "useless" simply *presupposes the English Banking-System*, under which a cash-business is denied to the people, and twenty pounds of interest-ridden monopoly-credit is superimposed upon one pound of actual money. This inflated, bank-note, bank-ledger "medium of exchange," is absolutely the most dishonest money possible to human beings. If Jevons, however, had put a probe into it—if he had not taken the entire abomination for granted—he would not have been orthodox as an English professor of his special day. He has been superseded at home by a better class of professors, and his chief wares are not worth a cent on our side of the Atlantic. The name of Cernuschi stands prominently, in a way, for bimetallism; yet even he set down the chief function of money to be the mere fad of "*international exchange*," and held that the re-monetization of silver in America, without European co-operation, more or less, would be an act of "*great audacity*." As if any country had ever depended on another for its government, its religion, or its system of money! If there were a pennyweight of brains in this fad, the thing for Americans to do, in this great republic, would be to *ask no questions of England*, for instance, but to establish *our own money*, and let England utter hers, in accordance with it. Why should *we* follow *her*? But all talk of "international money"—the real need of it, at least—is utter nonsense, and, *when honest*, verges on idiocy. The *only* use of an "international money" is to settle trade-balances between different countries, unless to furnish American dudes with a universal currency for their traveling expenses, as an inducement to keep them abroad. Whatever America buys of Europe is paid for, not in gold, but in corn, cotton, beef, pork, and our other American products, which are sold at *gold-prices* in London or Hamburg. And, in the present state of civilization, even *trade-balances* are largely closed in *bonds* and *stocks*. If they are American bonds or stocks, they are sold at *American values*, in *the money of the nation that buys them*. People in the United States who never saw a gold-piece, but who suppose they are "intelligent" because they can read the purchased opinions of

* "So with Michael Chevalier in 1850. First he wrote down gold and recommended its demonetization; then he turned the table upon silver. Now he is in doubt."—Ernest Seyd: letter to Samuel Hooper, February 17th, 1872.

some newspaper, talk till their teeth chatter about "all the gold going out of the country" and "our falling to a silver basis." It would be a great fall *upward*, as compared with our present position. Our old silver dollar again, under free-coinage, would at once raise the price of the metal beyond the possibility of England's buying an ounce of it for sixty or seventy cents, and putting that ounce of silver into two-and-a-half rupees, good in poor, innocent, swindled India for a bushel of wheat, with other products in proportion. Just this one thing, as we have said, makes a difference against the United States of nearly *a thousand millions of dollars a year*, out of which the gold-thugs and the Bank-Tories have bilked us. For the moment, too, their buccaneering has turned the balance of trade against us, which the silver dollar would restore. Then we could push the gold out of the country, to furnish more currency to buy our exports, and could yet command, from our own mines, precisely what amount of that metal we might need. Seeing this point—which is really clear and simple enough—Mr. Moreton Frewen—practically, perhaps, the keenest and most sincere financial expert of all present Englishmen—unhesitatingly declares that the United States, on a silver basis, would immediately become the most prosperous nation ever known to mankind. *It is true.* Still, there is no need of such a monetary basis. We are large producers of gold, *with* our silver; we require much more of both metals than we can possibly get, if we are ever to conduct our affairs dollar for dollar with a self-redeeming money. But what we can spare of both, safely substituting government paper, other countries want—are literally "dying for"—all their people except their knaves, and those who fiddle and drum for them.

On grounds of strict, Old-Testament justice—an eye for an eye, a tooth for a tooth—the only proper arguments against the Anglo-Tory gold-fiends would be starvation and death, with confiscation of their spoils. But American liberty, with law and order—the flower of modern civilization—simply cannot afford retaliation, except in self-defense. So our revenge must be with ballots, unless the conspirators and traitors themselves shall dare to step beyond the Constitution and the Laws—a case in which it will be our sacred duty to make short work with them. Meanwhile, my countrymen, waste no time in reading the stale commodities, called opinions and convictions, of their panders and parasites.

Alexander Hamilton said:*

"To annul the use of either of the metals as money is to abridge the quantity of circulating medium, and is liable to all the objections which arise from the comparison of the benefits of a full, with the evils of a scanty, circulation."

Thomas Jefferson, Hamilton's colleague in Washington's cabinet, said:†

"I concur with you that the unit must stand on both metals."

* Report to Congress on the Mint: 1791. † In a letter to Hamilton, Feb., 1792.

Albert Gallatin—standing second to Hamilton in the early financial history of the United States—said:*

"England, [in demonetising silver], has departed widely from known principles and from those which regulate a sound metallic currency. * * * Even if the precedent were good, it could not be conveniently adopted in the United States. * * * The American dollar, of 371¼ grains of pure silver, is *the unit of money* and *standard of value* on which *all public and private contracts are founded.*"

R. M. T. Hunter—thirteen years Chairman of the Finance Committee of the United States Senate—said:†

"The mischief would be great indeed, if all the world were to adopt one of the precious metals as the standard of value. To adopt gold alone would diminish the specie currency more than one-half; and the reduction the other way, should silver be taken as the only standard, would be large enough to prove highly disastrous to the human race."

William H. Crawford—our Secretary of the Treasury in 1820—said:

"All intelligent writers on currency agree that, when it is *decreasing* in amount, *poverty and misery must prevail.*"

Daniel Webster—a gentleman held until recently among Americans as a good deal higher authority than any economic immigrants—said:

"Gold and silver, at the rates fixed by Congress, constitute *the legal tender standard of value* in this country, and neither Congress nor any State has authority to establish *any other standard* or to *displace this.* The *legal-tender,* therefore, the *constitutional standard of value,* is established, and cannot be overthrown. To overthrow it would shake the whole system."‡

In 1876 a Monetary Commission was instituted by the Congress of the United States, to investigate the changed relations of gold and silver subsequent to 1873. On the demonetization of silver the Commission reported:

"This is a one-sided system, which can operate only in the interest of the security of the creditor, the usurer, and pawnbroker, whom it enables, through the falling prices which itself occasions, to swallow up the shrunken resources of the debtor, but is impotent to protect the interests of the unsecured business creditor, the debtor, or society, when, from any cause, the supply of the money metals becomes deficient. The world has expended a vast amount of labor in the production of the precious metals, has made great sacrifices in upholding the automatic metallic-system of money, and has a right to insist that it shall be consistently let alone to work out its own conclusions, or that it be abandoned."

* Views submitted at the request of the U. S. Treasury Department, Dec. 31, 1829.
† Report in 1859 on the act of creating a small silver-token currency, to keep silver-change in the country.
‡ By the demonetization of silver—"the crime of 1873"—as Hon. A. J. Warner declared some years ago in Faneuil Hall, "the constitutional standard *was* overthrown, and the whole system *was* shaken."

Of the Monetary Commission of 1876, Senator John P. Jones of Nevada was appointed Chairman, and Mr. George M. Weston, of Maine, was made Secretary. Both of these gentlemen became so absorbed in their work as to devote their lives to the study of Monetary Science. In his book on "The Silver Question," Mr. Weston has given the history of demonetization in all its main branches and connections. He has exposed and utterly wiped out the literary gold-dervishes of two continents. Among other things, Mr. Weston says:

"Theoretical and abstract discussions upon comparatively unimportant aspects of the question of the standards, become an unendurable impertinence, in presence of the plain fact that to attempt to make the small existing quantity of gold the sole metallic currency at one and the same time of Europe and the United States, must be fatal to labor and to every form of human possessions, excepting only money. * * * Demonetization augments, and was intended to augment, the burden of public and private debts, and is perhaps the most flagrant and audacious of the manifestations of the control exercised by foreign and domestic bankers over national legislation, in these recent and evil days."*

On the 12th and 13th of May, 1890—as the result of thirteen years of special study subsequent to his chairmanship of the Monetary Commission —Senator Jones delivered a two-days' speech in our National Capitol on "The Free Coinage of Silver," proving, from every standpoint known to discussion of the subject, the moral, political and financial need of the immediate restoration to that metal of the value filched from it by debased legislation. Senator Jones's speech is undoubtedly the most logical, comprehensive, and exhaustive parliamentary address on money, that had ever fallen from human lips, and is only equalled by his own great Senatorial address of 1893. These speeches remind one of the Mohammedan soldier who made a bonfire of the Alexandrian Library, saying that all its books of any account were in the Koran. With such documents to be had for the asking, it is pitiable that anybody in America seeking financial culture, should waste cerebration on some Jew-banker's public clerk called an "author," or some lawyer appointed by the gold-board of a college to fill the chair of Professor of Monopoly.

THE ROBBERY OF SILVER—the theft of its money-function—is but one topic, though a very important one, treated in this monograph, which, if not large or long, is in its way, the history of currency and banking. But I for one must say at the outset, that I regard any *instructed* person who opposes replacing the money of the United States in its precise legal form at the opening of 1873, as morally emasculated, and a dangerous character to an upright community. Whatever money is absolutely best, whatever money may prevail when science shall govern its ultimate form and substance, there is not much hope of any people who fail to RIGHT A WRONG, when they can do it, and to punish the perpetrators. The criminals of

* "The Silver Question," pages 102 and 106.

our Senate and House in 1873, who smuggled through their trustful lines the corpse of the silver-dollar, assassinated under cover and mask of a "Mint Act"—with the smell of an English bribe, too, on their hands—are not all of them now alive, and those who are may never go to the gallows or the prison they deserve. They may only be hanged in American history, and their names consigned to the bottom of Sheol. But the *character of their country can be vindicated by reversing their work.* Let it be done. Then it may be time to do something further in the same direction.

CHAPTER I.

WHAT IS MONEY?*

In answer to this question, a child, some "statesmen," and many traders, will say that money is gold, silver, and bank-bills, with copper or nickel coins for small transactions. Certainly it is. But, at different periods in the progress of mankind, it has been almost everything else.

SHEEP AND CATTLE WERE THE EARLIEST MONEY in general use to any large extent. In Sparta, where Lycurgus determined to breed a race of hardy soldiers, with few wants and no luxuries, he would have nothing but iron for his "medium of exchange"—a cart-load for ten dollars. In ancient Britain, slaves were used for coins, and were named "living money." Thus, the ancestors of Jay Gould, perhaps, were passed from hand to hand to buy pork.

When Rome first came to need a legal-tender, Servius Tullius coined copper, imprinting on the pieces images of domestic animals. These were the "gold basis" behind the fiat-tokens. Rome had no monetary use for gold until two centuries before the Christian era. She coined silver a little earlier. Her great rival, Carthage, used leather, turned into some form of treasury imprints. When Nicolo and Maffeo Polo went from Venice to Cathay, they found that money there consisted of the inner bark of a tree, cut in circles, bearing the stamp of the king. It was a very effective "legal tender"; for to counterfeit this money, or to refuse it, was death.

Glass-coin was once the currency of Arabia, and codfish the "gold-standard" of Newfoundland. Platinum was discontinued in Russia as late as 1845, and soap, at the Castle of Perota, in Mexico, after 1847. Africa, on occasion, passes strips of cotton-cloth as Bank-of-England notes, redeemable on demand in uses of modest adornment. Once, in Massachusetts, when Indians were numerous and lead was scarce, musket-balls became *money*, of the highest "intrinsic value." Gold was "a seventy-cent dollar" beside a bit of junk for bullets. In 1732, tobacco was a legal

* Senator Jones, in his great speech of May, 1890, has given, in tabular form, the substance of this chapter, and very much more, with all the authorities.

tender in Maryland, and tenpenny nails were the small-change of Scotland in 1776. Before the good Mr. George W. Childs converted Philadelphia into a large village-paradise, turnips circulated there instead of copper cents. It was as late as 1865, and Mr. Childs's own paper, the "Ledger," is authority for the fact.

But the line of history is long, not to say endless, on this subject. Almost every animal of human use, many vegetables and cereals, nearly all the metals, and a great variety of minerals, have been employed at different times, among different nations, to exchange commodities: that is to say, all these things have constituted money.

What then, again, is this thing? From facts alone, with no dependence on theory, we have already found the answer. Money is some generally recognized embodiment, or some legally-imposed certificate, of purchasing-power.

CHAPTER II.

GOLD AND SILVER AS MONEY.

Trade began in barter. If people's wants could be supplied in all instances by even exchanges of things wanted, there would be no need of money. But this being impossible in a state of civilized existence, some medium of all traffic is required—something which can atomize or aggregate, to any extent, the value of property. Gold and silver have been the most general means of accomplishing this purpose, ever since the days when Abraham bought a burial-place for Sarah, and "weighed to Ephon the silver which he had named in the audience." And as early, certainly, as the rise of the Macedonian empire, careful systems of coinage had superseded the necessity of weighing bits or bars of the "precious metals" with every transfer of merchandise. Governments had taken the matter in hand, and had stamped on the face of money the official recognition of its weight and worth.

There is no doubt that in very early times, gold and silver carried with them an approximation to what is ignorantly termed "INTRINSIC VALUE" —that is, purchasing-power pretty nearly uniform in different countries coming under "ancient civilization." And this point was a vital one. For ancient trade was a caravan quite as much as a shop. The great merchants were the universal travellers, who needed always on hand a universal currency. Again, as some government was tipped over every few years, a money founded on anything short of the direct occupancy of accepted value in its units was too uncertain an article to be trusted. It was best to have something which, in case of a nation's collapse, a subject could tie in his beard, or strap round his body, while he emigrated.

Thus, naturally and inevitably, gold and silver became "the world's money." But, WHEN MODERN COMMERCE AROSE, the precious metals, without reference to ratio between them, or anything else, were found to be *utterly insufficient to represent and exchange commodities.* So they were supplemented with *the vast systems of credit* which have since grown up on gold and silver as a "basis." The Jews of Lombardy, it is said, invented the "bill of exchange," to adjust trade between nations; and, for several centuries, markets and fairs were held, throughout Europe, at which merchants met, to balance accounts, in the absence of a currency to help them through. Then, later, banking arose.

CHAPTER III.

THE FIRST GREAT BANK.

It is a popular superstition of the most dangerous sort that an American "bank of issue" is a thing honestly resting on a metallic currency. The truth is that the modern banking-system owes its whole existence to the simple fact that no modern nation either *has*, or *can possibly get*, at any time, enough "specie"—whether gold, or silver, or both—*to do an honest cash-business.* This was THE FIRST REASON FOR BANK-PAPER, and has always been the chief meaning of it. Moreover, the only bank on the globe that ever operated on a vast scale, with perfect consistency, perfect satisfaction, and long-continued success, completely ignored that implement of inflation, contraction and suspension, commonly known as a "specie basis" with "redemption on demand." This was THE BANK OF VENICE, to which the Bank of France is now, in effect, the nearest approximation.

The Bank of Venice was the one great clearing-house of Europe's commercial metropolis in the middle and early-modern ages.* It was instituted in 1171, on loans to the government by wealthy citizens, compelled by the exigencies of war. The government needing supplies, the reigning Doge demanded subscriptions to a fund of two million ducats. The subscribers to the fund were appointed managers of it, and the State agreed to pay four per cent. annual interest on it. The capital was made divisible and transferable on the books of the bank, and this feature constituted the stock a medium of exchange—money. The government fixed no time to repay the loans; but the bank soon became so strong, popular and necessary, that no one desired they should ever be paid. They became simply so much capital of the nation, invested in a great, cheap tool—a currency of sufficient volume to meet the requirements of Venetian trade. New subscriptions were offered, and were accepted to the limits of the public debt. As this increased, the capital of the bank slowly accumulated

---

* Its history, here condensed, is elaborately given in Colwell's "Ways and Means of Payment." J. P. Lippincott & Co., Publishers, 1859.

through six hundred years, until it finally reached some fourteen million ducats.

The advantages of the bank to the whole Venetian people soon became so apparent that the government abolished the payment of interest on the loans. The divisible stock was merely converted into a legal-tender for debts, public and private, and all bills of exchange, with no specification to the contrary, were made payable at this one great center of circulation, which so facilitated and stimulated every branch of business, then existing, that the bank-inscriptions sometimes ranged at *thirty per cent. above par in gold*, and had to be limited finally by law to a *premium of twenty per cent.*

Coin always flowed into the bank in abundance, WITH NO PROMISE OF SPECIE REDEMPTION. It was taken by the State, once and for good. But it was immediately paid out for State-expenses, and thus turned directly back into the smaller currents of trade, while the bank-inscriptions floated the wholesale transactions, both of government and people. Occasionally, coin was required in large quantities, for export; and, in exceptional instances, the demand for it rose beyond that of the bank-credits. In such instances, the holders gladly pushed it off their hands, at whatever small advance they could get, knowing that the vast industries of Venice would soon call it back, as surely as the Venetian sun would draw moisture from the earth and the sea. Then the gold would be a drug in the market again, as it usually was, and a profit would be certain on the rise of the inscriptions in bank. There was no chance, however, for much speculation in coin, as a margin on it was too rare and insignificant to demand any great attention. The large margins, on the other hand, were always *against the coin*, and had to be limited at last, as we have seen, by law.

And now, what were the general results of this system of banking? For one thing, there was no commercial crisis—NOT ONE MONEY-PANIC IN VENICE for six hundred years. History has no hint of such a thing. The State had *solved the problem of trade*—had furnished a sufficient medium of exchange to transfer the world's commodities with perfect ease and rapidity. Combined with the industry and enterprise of her citizens, her great bank placed her at the head of the material wealth and prosperity of Europe, and held her there for ages. When Buonaparte conquered Italy, the Bank of Venice fell with the State. But the invader gained nothing by it—no gold, no silver, no riches that *he* could utilize. He simply destroyed the credit of an institution that had stood spotless and perfect for six centuries.

As the capital-stock of the Bank of Venice was, at the maximum, about sixteen millions of dollars, was divisible, and was the chief medium of exchange for the products of Europe and Asia, it might, if necessary, have been transferred on the ledgers of the bank dozens of times a day, and thus have served as a currency with a volume of several hundred millions.* During the bank's long existence, it saved *many times its entire capital* in the mere *wear and tear of metal* alone. But all such negative items are too trivial to mention, as compared with the magnificent positive gains attending A REALLY "HONEST" SYSTEM OF MONEY—gold and silver, supplemented with direct government credit. During those six hundred years, that wonderful bank made, for the Venetian people, thousands of times its investment and cost. In short, the facility of transfer afforded by its legal tenders made *Venetian commerce itself* the thing it was—made Venice *the entrepot and depot of the civilized world*. Venetian prosperity was the offspring of Venetian money. The one could never have been without the other.

CHAPTER IV.

SHYLOCK'S BANK OF ENGLAND.†

Let us now look at another bank, as it stands in the history of two hundred years—THE BANK OF ENGLAND. This gigantic weapon of aristocracy and oppression, which has become the most cruel, hypocritical and dangerous monopoly on earth, was established on the first of January, 1695, upon a loan of six millions of dollars to the English government. Interest on the loan was secured to the stockholders by specified taxation, and they were paid twenty thousand dollars a year for handling the fund. The institution was chartered as a bank of deposit, loan and discount. It had no direct authority to emit notes as currency, but assumed the right as implicit in its charter, and inaugurated the custom of exchanging its own paper, PROMISING SPECIE ON DEMAND, for the time-notes of individuals and business establishments. As a *mere matter of method*, these authenticated certificates of the Bank of England were an improvement on the divisible credit-inscriptions of the Bank of Venice; for printed acknowledgments of value in hand are more convenient for circulation than ledger-accounts and written receipts for funds in bank. But, in discounting paper due in the future, and substituting for it promises to pay coin on demand, the Bank of England became the real parent of "MODERN SPECULATION," though she has always tried to palm off the brat on everybody else. She quickly begat, also, four other ugly daughters,

---

* "It is not improbable that the whole fund of the bank performed payments in the aggregate, annually, to five hundred and perhaps a thousand fold the amount."—Colwell, page 302.

† The information contained in this chapter can be found in Colwell's "Ways and Means of Payment," Alison's "History of Europe," and Doubleday's "Financial, Monetary and Statistical History of England." These authorities were followed by John C. Calhoun, in his great Senatorial Money-Speech of October 3d, 1837, and are accurately quoted, to a considerable extent, in Berkey's "Money Question," a book easily procured. Pounds have here been put into dollars, one to five.

named INFLATION, CONTRACTION, SUSPENSION, and GENERAL BANKRUPTCY. Their photographs have been already placed in the rogue's-gallery of this album.

There is not one fifth—many authorities declare there is not really one tenth—of the gold and silver in existence, for the exchanges of commerce requiring cash. Still, this commerce demands, and *must have*, some medium of exchange. So the public pressed the Bank of England for circulation, and, to furnish it, the bank solemnly guaranteed, on the face of its issues, to overcome the limits of nature and surpass the bounties of God. Such is always, and necessarily, the promise of an inflated bank-bill on a "specie-basis." It is the money of complete atheism and unavoidable rascality.

Was it the deliberate purpose of the Government of England, and of the corporators of her official bank, to use this institution for A UNIVERSAL CONFIDENCE-GAME? At the outset, no. The plan of issuing bank-notes redeemable in coin, and then inflating the paper five or ten times beyond the very physical possibility of keeping the promise—this athletic jump at the moon was not originally a trick of English dishonesty, but only a bungle of English stupidity. It was hoped and believed that the bank-notes would be so convenient and necessary, in general trade, that only a fraction of them would ever be presented for redemption *at one time*. And such may be the case while the stream of commerce is unruffled—while peace and prosperity ride on it. But, the moment these are disturbed—as they *must* soon be disturbed in the process of setting a financial cone on its apex—that moment "public confidence is shaken," and there is a "run on specie." The specie being never sufficient for a run, the end is always "a panic."

Thus the Bank of England, starting with the amiable fraud of a specie basis for an inflated credit currency, has been the most stupendous repudiator of its obligations, and, strictly speaking, the most *destructive failure* of the modern world. The bank itself is rich enough, no doubt; but to say that for every pound sterling of its stockholders' profits it has destroyed ten thousand pounds of other people's wealth—this statement would fall so far short of the actual, terrible truth, that no rigid computation need be attempted. Yet even this result is not in one sense the worst. Once the policy of the bank, as we have seen, was only A BLUNDER, and could be pardoned; but now this same policy HAS BECOME A CRIME—a deliberate scheme to aid England in robbing the human race, the mass of her own subjects included, in the interest of the intelligent, shrewd, but selfish and unscrupulous aristocracy of the kingdom.

The government of Great Britain has no respect, no compassion for the poor and ignorant. It has squeezed the life out of Ireland, out of India, out of Egypt—out of every race of human beings that are cursed with its domination. In the name of Christianity and civilization, it imbrutes and impoverishes the whole world, as far as possible, that English greed may rule the land and the sea; and then it hoodwinks and fleeces the millions of its own subjects at home, that one royal family and some thirty thousand landed, titled cormorants, may shine in gold and satin, and dine on grouse and brandy. For nearly a hundred years, the Bank of England has been a special partner and a ready tool in this diabolism. Virtually, the government winks at the bank, the bank winks at the government, and the two join hands to pillage the globe.

Let us take the most notable instance on record—that of 1797.*

Britain was then at war with Buonaparte. The gold and silver of the kingdom had been rapidly withdrawn, and the bank had only about five millions of dollars left. The bank went through the form of consulting the government, and the government ordered the bank to "suspend specie payments." THE SUSPENSION LASTED TWENTY-FIVE YEARS—until Waterloo ended the career of Napoleon. During that time, the necessities of British royalty and British aristocracy forced them to give the whole nation *honest money*, which means a sufficient circulating-medium to call forth all the ingenuity and industry of production and trade. Paper money, on the principle of the Bank of Venice, was substituted for the insane and mendacious promises of specie on demand. What was the consequence? Why, exactly what is always the consequence when all the people of a country have a fair chance *to work*. For a quarter of a century, England was as prosperous, in spite of her great wars, as Venice had been, for five centuries, in like circumstances. In 1797, the public revenue was a hundred and fifteen millions of dollars. In 1815, it had easily been raised to three hundred and sixty millions. The lowest annual collection from loans and taxes was two hundred and thirty-six millions, and in 1813 it reached five hundred and forty millions. The suspended bank borrowed for the government seventeen hundred and fifty millions. Three million acres of waste land were improved and cultivated; and the exportation of the single class of articles comprised in cotton manufactures increased from thirty-five millions of dollars, in 1801, to a hundred and thirty-five millions, in 1822. And, for this one quarter of a century, there was NO COMMERCIAL CRASH, NO RUN ON THE BANK, NO MONEY-PANIC. The great land-owners, the great stock-and-bond jobbers, the great bullion-loaners, did not *want* a money crisis: it was *not for their interest* to have one, and be eaten up, pound, shilling and pence, by the French.

But as soon as Waterloo assured the continuation of European king-craft, with its various oligarchies and monopolies, the aristocratic wealth and intelligence of Great Britain combined to rob the poor and ill-informed classes, whose labor and commercial activity had saved the realm. To the enormous industries which an adequate system of money had called into being, a sufficiency of circulation had now become as much a necessity,

* Alison's History of Europe gives all this with copious and minute detail. Doubleday is also full and elaborate.

in exchanging merchandise, as a sufficiency of trucks and boats to transfer the merchandise from place to place. If the king and parliament had "called in" three quarters of all the vehicles of transportation, and prohibited the use of them, the value of every great commercial staple would of course have shrunk into insignificance; while the few persons having a monopoly of trucks and boats—say one certain kind, with gilded sterns and tail-boards—would have been able to command, and buy up at a song, the property of other people. But the British masses would have understood this measure, and, in spite of stolidity and beer, would have answered it with a whirlwind of destruction. So A MORE SUBTILE AND COWARDLY METHOD was adopted to accomplish *precisely the same result*. A parliamentary act was passed, under the whip of the stock-gambling Ricardo, *to resume specie payments*—which meant simply to withdraw from use the larger part of the monetary facilities of commercial exchange.* Inevitably, the result was the most stupendous crash in business, the most cruel wreck of a people's property, the most murderous impoverishment of innocent labor, that had ever taken place in modern times. Producers, manufacturers, merchants, were ruined by thousands, and workmen were dropped into idleness by tens of thousands CRIME WAS NECESSITATED AT WHOLESALE by law and order, and THEN PUNISHED AT RETAIL by the same forces that were the real projectors of it. Revolution was threatened, was begun, and was finally suppressed by military force. Even the revenue of the kingdom was cut down below the possibility of reducing the public debt. But *the few who held bullion* or were rich enough to stand the strain, *swiftly increased their possessions*, and forty-thousand powerful owners of real-estate absorbed a hundred and ten thousand weaker ones.

It was the most diabolical invasion of English welfare since William of Normandy, with his brigands in mail, had landed at Hastings. As far as the British *masses* were concerned, they could have lost little if anything more, had Buonaparte been permitted to take the island. And THIS WAS THE WORK OF THE ENGLISH BANK-SYSTEM, though dominated by the same merciless spirit as that of the more extended money-power which has nearly wrecked both Europe and America in our own day. The "specie basis" was simply a slung-shot and sand-bag, with which to sneak behind the honest workers of the realm, and do them to death. By use of this peculiar bludgeon, a few of Ricardo's hebraic gold-bugs, in league with the titled descendants of those who conquered the country in 1066, gobbled up the fruits of its progress without the trouble of resort to arms, which was the more manly method of the Norman pirates, if not of Jacob when he cheated Isaac and Esau.†

* The contraction of the actual *currency* was about forty per cent. The contraction of *discounts*—the "elastic" banking frauds of the British thimble-rig—was nine dollars of every ten.
† The directors of the Bank of England themselves protested, in this instance, against contraction. But their established system choked them. Ricardo said it would be a matter of "three per cent" in the "fall of prices."

In 1844, the ruin that the Bank of England had so often wrought, compelled the passage of an act by the government limiting the currency-notes of the bank to the actuality of redemption in government securities and coin. But the system was at once so utterly bad and so thoroughly fixed, that the "bank-act" did little good. The institution kept on with the OLD DODGE IN ANOTHER WAY. Discounts of commercial paper, entered on its books, took the place of inflated notes by its issue-department. But these discounts, too, called largely for gold: so, when the least drain on the metal-vaults began, discounts were shut off, interest was raised, doubled, quadrupled, and property of all sorts was dumped on the market, to pay gold to the bank for the discounted paper. Then the industrial world went to pieces, as usual. As American banks have been nothing but a retinue of the Bank of England—promising coin on paper inflations—*their credits, too,* have been "*called in,*" as soon as their London mother has begun, from any cause, to drain away their metal. Thus, *every six years* prior to 1861, and several times since, the people of the United States have been a dish of oysters for John Bull.*

In October of 1875, the New York Board of Trade was addressed, at their invitation, by General Butler. Referring to the Bank of England, he said:

"What a marvel of financial strength and credit she has been, to be sure! Well may the bullionists sing pæans to this *destructionist of all values for their benefit!*"

When General Butler stigmatized the Bank of England as "the destructionist of all values," he hit the mark exactly. The phrase sums up the whole history of that huge financial blood-sucker.

CHAPTER V.

OUR COLONIAL MONEY.

It would fill a cyclopædia to estimate and describe the wickedness, the poverty and misery, which the British banking-policy, and those who live by its wreckage, have wrought in America. So far as control by it could be forced upon the Colonies, before the Revolution, it was an unmitigated curse to them, and it has been an ever-recurring stroke of paralysis from the beginning to the end of our history.

The early colonists of the United States exchanged their productions and property chiefly through the primitive means of barter. The little gold and silver brought with them from Europe was quickly sent back to procure the ordinary necessities of civilized life. The few exports were

* Our home Shylocks, of course, have had a large spoon in it—the chief spoon; but the *English* system has wrought the wreck. Berkey has compiled the facts very well. See his "Money Question."

turned to the same account. Coin could not be kept in the country, though various attempts were made to retain it.* THE FIRST LEGAL TENDER established by Massachusetts was the beads of the Indians, called wampum; and, as far as it went, it answered the purpose of money quite as well as English gold or Spanish silver.

But, six years before the Bank of England was instituted, the infant colony made a paper-issue to pay her soldiers who had been sent on an expedition against Canada. The issue was for seven thousand pounds, in notes from five shillings to five pounds, redeemable in taxes—that is, in the inevitable debts of those who held the paper, and of all citizens who owned property. Let us glance at the form of one of these notes :†

"This indented bill of ten shillings, due from the Massachusetts colony to the possessor, shall be in value equal to money, and shall be accordingly accepted by the treasurer and receivers subordinate to him, in all public payments, and for any stock (cattle) at any time in the treasury."

The colony notes, we observe, were not made a legal tender—not stamped as money to pay private debts; but in 1692 it was ordered that they should be received by the treasury at five per cent over coin. This "fiat" brought them at once to par with gold, and they stayed there for twenty years, until taken up in the revenues of the colony. Similar, but larger issues, were subsequently authorized, as the only way to furnish a currency and promote the growth of the province. In 1773 the whole people of Massachusetts were in a prosperous condition, and the colony was out of debt.

OTHER COLONIES—Connecticut, New York, Pennsylvania, Maryland, Delaware—issued the same kind of bills, at about the same time. In 1755 Virginia put out her notes to sustain the war of that period, and guaranteed their redemption in a specific tax. To make sure of success, the notes bore five per cent interest. Their history was afterward written by the same hand that drafted the Declaration of Independence—the hand of THOMAS JEFFERSON.‡ "Not a bill of this emission," said he, "was found in circulation." And why? It was so popular and well-accredited that "it was locked up in the chests of executors, guardians, widows, farmers." We "then issued bills bottomed on a redeeming tax, but bearing no interest. These were received, and never depreciated a single farthing."

The history of another issue of Colonial money has been given by BENJAMIN FRANKLIN. In his statement to the British Board of Trade in 1764, Dr. Franklin said that in 1723 Pennsylvania had been "totally stripped of its gold and silver," the "chief part of the trade being carried on by the extremely inconvenient method of barter." But, "paper

* For details consult "Sumner's History of American Currency," and "Historical Sketches of American Paper Currency," by Henry Phillips, Jr., A. M.
† See address by Charles Sumner, U. S. Senate, Feb. 13th, 1862.
‡ Letter to John W. Eppes, June 24th, 1813.

money" being "first made there," gave "new life to business, promoted greatly the settlement of new lands, whereby the province has so greatly increased in inhabitants that the export from thence thither is more than ten fold what it was."

The record of still another issue of Colonial money has been left to us in the eloquence of JOHN C. CALHOUN. On the 18th of September, 1837, pressing the issue of United States treasury notes, to relieve the government and the people then floundering in *a general bank-suspension*, Mr. Calhoun said:

"It is my impression that, in the present condition of the world, a paper currency is almost indispensable in financial and commercial operations of civilized and extensive communities. In many respects it has a vast superiority over a metallic currency, especially in great and extended transactions, by its greater cheapness, lightness, and the facility of determining the amount. * * * It may throw some light on the subject to state that North Carolina, just after the Revolution, issued a large amount of paper, which was made receivable in dues to her; it was also made a legal tender, but which, of course, was not obligatory after the adoption of the Federal Constitution. A large amount, say between four and five hundred thousand dollars, remained in circulation after that period, and continued to circulate, for more than twenty years, at par with gold and silver during the whole time, with no other advantage than being received in the revenue of the State, which was much less than one hundred thousand dollars."

It would be interesting to extend our information of this kind, derived from the great founders of American institutions, and the early statesmen of the republic. But a word must suffice. It was no "gold standard," it was no bank-paper, but it was government-issues, good for public revenue, and aided chiefly by a little silver, that nourished, and stimulated the growth of the thirteen American colonies into a condition to defy England and achieve their independence.

In 1763 the British Parliament declared all colonial acts for the issue of paper currency to be void. "Every medium of exchange," said the British Board of Trade, "should have an intrinsic value, which paper has not." Dr. Franklin there and then exploded this bosh—more than a century and a quarter ago—though many parrots are still repeating it.

"However fit," [said Franklin],* "a particular thing may be for a particular purpose, whenever that thing is not to be had, or not to be had in sufficient quantity, it becomes necessary to use something else, the fittest thing that can be got in lieu of it. Bank bills and banker's notes are in daily use here [in London], as a medium of trade, yet they have no intrinsic value, but rest on the credit of those that issued them, as paper bills in the colonies do on the credit of the respective settlements there. * * * Being payable in cash upon sight by the drawers is indeed a circumstance that cannot attend the colony bills, their cash being drawn from them by the British trade; but the legal tender being instituted, is rather *a greater advantage* to the possessor, since he need not be at the trouble of going to a particular bank or banker to demand the money." "At this very time," [continued Franklin], "the silver money in England

* Works: Duane's edition, 1809, vol. 4, page 87.

is obliged to the legal tender for a part of its value—that part which is the difference between its real weight and its denomination. Great part of the shillings and sixpences now current, are, in wearing, become five, ten, twenty, and some of the sixpences even fifty per cent too light. For this difference between the real and nominal you have no intrinsic value; you have not so much as paper; you have nothing. *It is the legal tender, with the knowledge that it can easily be repassed for the same value, that makes three penny worth of silver pass for six pence.*"

The REAL OBJECTION, of course, to COLONIAL PAPER MONEY on the part of England, was the fear it would render the colonies *too independent of British rule and the British money-power*. Dr. Franklin's unanswerable common-sense was wasted on the buccaneers of the gold-pot, just as all truth is wasted on them now. But, a dozen years after his protest, came the battle of Bunker Hill and the CONTINENTAL ARMY; and with these came "CONTINENTAL MONEY."

Continental money, as Mr. Calhoun said, in the greatest of his financial speeches,* "*is a ghost that is ever conjured up by all who wish to give the banks an exclusive monopoly of government credit.*" But those who are not grossly ignorant of American history know well enough that Continental money was a remarkably effective weapon for its purpose, and that, considering its results, it was the best investment for the human family, that was ever made, in any country or in any age.† American Patriots—those who whipped both the Red-Coats and the Tories by its aid, and then bore the losses connected with it—rejoiced rather than whined over them. That same immortal pen, again, which drafted the Declaration of Independence and the Constitution of Virginia, has summed up this matter in a way to leave nothing open for argument.‡

"Continental money" [says Jefferson] 'expired without a groan. Not a murmur was heard among the people. On the contrary, universal congratulation took place on their seeing the gigantic mass quietly interred in its grave. Foreigners, indeed, have been loud, and still are loud, in their complaints. A few of them have reason; but the most noisy are not the best. They are persons who have become bankrupt by unskillful attempts at commerce with America. That they may have some pretext to offer to their creditors, they have bought up great masses of this dead money of America, where it is to be had at five thousand for one, and they show the certificates of their paper possessions, as if they had died in their hands and had been the cause of their bankruptcy."

---

* Oct. 3d, 1837.

† To bankers and bullionists, John Sherman is now their great authority on money—for considerations mutually satisfactory. But, on the 13th of February, 1862, this same John Sherman said in the Senate: "*I much prefer the credit of the United States, based as it is upon all the productions and property of the United States, to the issues of any corporation, however well guaranteed and managed.* * * * The only objection to the issue of this paper money [the greenbacks] is that too many may be issued. * * * If, in our Revolutionary war, the amount of the Revolutionary scrip, and in the French Revolution the amount of assignats, had been confined to a small sum in proportion to the wealth of the country,—if, for instance, it had been limited to one tenth of the annual production of the country—there would have been no danger.*"

‡ Jefferson's Works, vol. V, page 249.

At the commencement of the Revolution the population of the thirteen Colonies was two millions and a half, and their property six hundred millions of dollars. They had five millions of dollars in specie. On such a basis, Congress issued, during the war, about two hundred millions of dollars in bills of credit—a third of the whole property of the country—and these were *counterfeited*, without stint, by the British defenders of "*honest money*," that they might help their Hessian mercenaries to defeat Washington and his army.

But *what was* this continental money, the remembrance of which has stricken so many misers with ague and grip? It was no "fiat-money"—no accredited paper of a strong government, redeemable in revenue, at a fixed standard of value, and held at par by limit of volume. "Continental money," on the contrary, was issued according to *the approved tenets of the Specie Basis.* The bills promised to pay, a few years from date, their face, *with interest*, in "Spanish milled dollars." They were emitted on the authority of the several States, with the indorsement of Congress that the United States would "insure the payment," and would "draw bills of exchange, annually, if demanded." The fulfillment of these promises was impossible. They were made in good faith, and with the hope of speedy success for the American army. For a year, the bills circulated at par with silver, and in their third year the premium on the coin was only seventy-five per cent. But, as the struggle continued, the people came to realize the huge joke of attempting to redeem, "in Spanish milled dollars," an amount of paper, genuine and counterfeit, calling for more than fifty times the whole sum of coin in the country, and counting interest, three or four hundred times the sum of the coin specified in the promises. Still, the paper circulated; and the determined, patriotic people kept passing it from hand to hand, as it went down, buying and selling with it—receiving it for *something*—until 1781. It then sank out of sight at a depreciation of five hundred per cent., but "with indulgence for its memory," said Jefferson, "as a thing which had vindicated the liberties of the country" and "fallen in the moment of victory." In other words, the American people came to regard the loss on Continental money—a loss borne by the whole of them—as *a general tax on their property, to secure American independence.* Thus the losers were not cheated. It was *they*, in fact, who insisted on letting their losses go, and would sanction no attempt to recover them. Congress did its best to fulfill its pledges, but the people laughed away every effort to fund or redeem the currency, and "barbers papered their shops with it." For once we got the better of British bullionists and counterfeiters.

CHAPTER VI.

THE ENGLISH SPAWN, OUR "OLD STATE-BANKS."

THE AMERICAN REVOLUTION was one of those fortunate occasions, in the world's annals, when selfishness joined hands with patriotism, greed with philanthropy, to do a great work. But, the work done, such elements could no longer be held together. There were thousands of inborn Tories among the nominal Whigs who aided in achieving American independence. England interfered with their *interests*, and they fought against her. But as soon as free from her rule themselves, they sought to adopt her various systems of tyranny and monopoly, to elevate and enrich themselves at the expense of the people. One of these adoptions was her system of banking, which, in order to live and grow, every one of the Colonies had been obliged partly to dodge and partly to reject. Some of those aristocratic patriots were perfectly frank in expressing their views.

ALEXANDER HAMILTON was the first Secretary of the United States Treasury. He was a great and honorable man. But he had little faith in democratic institutions. In 1787 he said:*

"I believe the British government forms the best model the world has ever produced. * * * All communities divide themselves into the few and the many. The first are the rich and well-born; the other, the mass of the people."

Even before the formation of the Constitution, Hamilton declared that the country had already begun "*to tire of an excess of democracy.*"

Such a man would naturally urge the establishment, in America, of a virtual supplement to the Bank of England. He was the father of THE BANK OF THE UNITED STATES—the earlier corporation of that name, which, in 1791, was chartered for twenty years, with a capital of ten million dollars. The younger Pitt—the long-headed Prime Minister of England—is said to have prophesied a little in regard to it, the prophecy being this:*

"Let the Americans adopt their funding system and go into their banking institutions, and *their independence will be a mere phantom.*"

From that day to this, we have been illustrating the point of the astute English statesman. What was American trade, American property, practical American welfare, from 1789 to 1861? And what has it been again in the spider's parlor—the well-woven "monetary stringency" of 1893? Our whole financial situation is nothing but a tail hitched to a kite—the gold of the Bank of England. When this kite has been "pulled in," the ridiculous tail has always followed—*to the ground.*

* "Debates of the Constitutional Convention." Yates, page 135.
† "Money Question." Berkey, page 303.

When our thirteen original States came under the compact of the Constitution, they turned over to the Federal Government all power of instituting money, as all of them desired to secure a sound and uniform currency. Thus the States were expressly debarred from "coining money," emitting "bills of credit," or making anything but gold and silver coin a tender in payment of debts. Congress was empowered to "borrow money on the credit of the United States," and, as no nation can negociate a loan without a formal promise to pay, the right to issue certificates of indebtedness was implied in the compact, while a specific proposition to vest the government with power to issue "bills of credit" was defeated. At the same time, it was understood and expressly declared by the framers of the Constitution, that, in case of war, or to meet any other great national requirement, the government could issue acknowledgments of value received from the people, redeemable in taxes, provided and secured by these same people. This is the *Constitutional basis* of the TREASURY NOTE, as elaborately explained by John C. Calhoun, following the lead of Franklin, Adams, Jefferson and Jackson, and as established by the various decisions of our Supreme Court.

As the Federal Government was denied by its founders the constitutional power to "emit bills of credit," and as the States were expressly prohibited from doing so, what right had either *to delegate a power which neither possessed*, to any corporation? When Hamilton's illegitimate Bank of the United States was conceived, Jefferson was Secretary of State. He opposed it with all his might. So did Madison in Congress. In 1811, when it applied for a renewal of its charter, Congress denied the application. The bank was pronounced "unconstitutional, anti-American," and strictly "*a British institution.*"

But, as Franklin had said, a civilized people *must* have some system of money, whether good or bad, constitutional or unconstitutional, if they are to exchange their productions, and are to grow at all in wealth. There *never had been coin enough* in America, and *never could be*, to represent her transfers of property. Such being the practical fact, Jefferson, Adams, Madison, Jackson, and those early statesmen of the republic who were *true to the people*, endeavored to furnish them a money measured by the gold and silver dollar, but at *normal volume*—the addition being made of government taxes, *the people's own inevitable debts to themselves.* Such money is the United States Treasury Note, as the only honest supplement to gold and silver coin.

As explained some way back, an inflated bank-issue, promising redemption in gold, is a thing that, in the structure of the earth, GOD AND NATURE HAVE MADE A LIE. But a treasury-note is a certificate to the holder that, for value received by the United States, he possesses purchasing power equal to that of coin, and corresponding to the face of his certificate, which is good for all his taxes, for every other man's taxes, and for all dues to the government. Treasury-notes, therefore, held by the people, are redeemable in the people's own obligations,—obligations which they *must* incur, if they exist as a nation. Such money is its own security. It has no need to go to any Hebrew junk-box for redemption. It is, in fact, nothing but a constant adjustment of balances between a government and its citizens.

THE FATHERS OF AMERICAN DEMOCRACY were foiled in their aim to bless the people with such a money. Independence achieved and peace established, society segregated into the various oligarchies which have since ruled the country. We have heard a great deal about the "Southern oligarchy of slaveholders." But the banking oligarchy of the North, the manufacturing oligarchies, the railway, tariff and party oligarchies,— these colossal and secretive forces have cramped and stripped the ignorant masses on every hand, depressing them as nearly as possible into beasts of burden. Meanwhile, with some glorious exceptions, the brassy and blatant "American press" has been owned and controlled by the same oligarchies; while the pulpit, once the natural defender of the poor and needy, has been everywhere intimidated, whenever its influence, now grown rather effeminate, has possessed intelligence enough to instruct and aid us.

Hamilton's illegitimate Bank of the United States was soon extinguished as unconstitutional. But, immediately after the Revolution, the various States were taken in hand by the MONEY-POWER, which easily found a way to render its own interests constitutional enough for all practical purposes, without regard to any principles laid down in parchments. The States granted charters to banks of issue so rapidly that for one bank in the country in 1781 there were one hundred in 1815. Twenty-five charters were issued by the legislature of Pennsylvania in 1813, but were vetoed by the Governor. The next session of that persevering legislature passed a bill over the veto, chartering forty-one banks, with a capital of seventeen millions of dollars. Thirty-seven of them got into operation at once, and then *suspended specie payments.*

But there is no need to follow, in detail, the villainous and ridiculous record of our Anglo-American State Banks. Almost their chief business was to "suspend," as soon as really called on to meet their obligations. It was impossible for them to avoid it:—they were *founded on that principle.* From 1809 to 1861 they suspended specie payments TEN TIMES, or ONCE IN FIVE YEARS. The Eastern banks were of course better than the "wild-cat" species of the West and South-West; yet the Commissioners' report of the banks of Connecticut, for example, from 1837 to 1849, shows that their average loans and discounts were more than *eleven and a half millions a year,* while their average specie was less than FOUR HUNDRED AND EIGHTY THOUSAND. They carried a debt, *payable on demand in coin,* twenty-four times as large as the amount of coin to pay it. Their financial pyramid was *one inch* square at the bottom, and *two* *feet* square at the top.* But *these* were "good, sound banks," in pretty "good times." In 1809, the Farmers' Exchange Bank of Gloucester, Rhode Island, was found to have nearly SIX HUNDRED THOUSAND DOLLARS of its bills afloat, and *eighty-six dollars of coin* for their specie basis. Here was a pyramid which measured *one square* INCH at the bottom and *fifty square* FEET at the top.†

✓The Chief Designers, however, made no mistake in this architecture. They *intended* that their structures should fall down frequently, but should fall on innocent and ignorant industry, which would thus be crushed, but the ruins of which would be picked up by the rich, to make them richer. AMERICAN BANKERS, in short, had now thoroughly learned all the tricks of their trans-Atlantic partners, THE GREAT CONFIDENCE-MEN OF THE BANK OF ENGLAND. For a hundred years the two sets of "operators" have conducted the most consummate swindle on earth. A few intelligent observers have long understood it, and have now and then exposed it. But the poor wretches who constitute the "masses of the people" have only just begun to comprehend its enormous wickedness.

CHAPTER VII.

THE SHYLOCK "PATRIOTS" OF 1861.

In 1861, when the Civil War broke out in the United States, a vigorous attempt was made, by some of the greatest Americans then living, to do away, for the time, with the British money-system in this country, and to cut loose from the apron-string of the Bank of England.

IT WAS A STRANGE YEAR IN AMERICA—the year 1861. It was an utter surprise, in a thousand ways, to everybody. Garrison and Phillips, with their band of ultra Abolitionists, had been at work, for a quarter of a century, filling the public mind with the moral necessity of emancipating the negro slaves of the Southern States. The agitation had re-acted, until the whole slave-holding interest had become belligerent and aggressive. The Plutocracy of the North—both the direct money-power and the leading commercial elements—had bent to the ground and licked the dust, to assure the South that anti-slavery was a momentary fanaticism, reprobated by all respectable and influential persons, who desired nothing but quiet, cotton and Southern trade, and who would relinquish any commandment of heaven or law of earth, to keep the peace. The anti-slavery sentiment, however, had grown among the people, as a whole, until it was adopted in a political form by the Republican Party, and sent

* Labor and Capital—A New Monetary System, &c.: by Edward Kellogg. See, also, Berkey.
† Sumner's History of American Currency, Henry Holt & Co., Pub's, 1874, page 62.

Lincoln to Washington. Still, the North was but partly awake, and was willing to "compromise" on almost anything. All it asked was that the civilization of South Carolina should not actually supplant that of Massachusetts on Northern soil, and that the Federal Union should not be dissolved. But the South was in earnest, and meant war for slavery. She fired on the flag at Sumpter.

No cannon ever met such response. Seeing the matter at last as it was, THE WHOLE NORTH AROSE IN AN INSTANT.* Democrat clasped hands with Republican; the most conservative "Silver-Grey" with the most radical Abolitionist. "Wide-Awakes" and "Little-Giants" threw down the torch and banner of political opposition, shouldered the gun instead, and marched side by side to Washington. The very "short-boys" and "dead-rabbits" of New York City grew wild with patriotism—even the "dangerous classes" burning, for the moment, to be dangerous alone to those who defied and insulted the American flag. The plain, honest people of the "Free States" committed themselves as one man to the war, putting life, property, everything they had, behind it. Then the Shylock brigade of Northern "gold-bugs" marched to Washington also. They went there TO GAIN CONTROL OF THE NATIONAL FINANCES and to MAKE MONEY OUT OF THE PEOPLE'S BLOOD AND TEARS.

The leader, then, of the House of Representatives, was THADDEUS STEVENS—one of the most powerful minds that ever dominated a public body, in any age or country. A lawyer, a statesman, a scholar, he was thoroughly informed both in the history of his country and its practical affairs. He had given special attention to the subject of finance—its ancient and modern systems. And the "great commoner" not only understood money, but he had *no desire to steal it*. In that terrible emergency of '61, he was, beyond all doubt, the ablest and best man in America for the position he held.†

Salmon P. Chase had been selected by Mr. Lincoln for Secretary of the Treasury. He was a lawyer, an orator, a prominent leader in the Anti-Slavery Movement, an experienced politician of the better class, and a man of large and deserved influence, especially in his own State, Ohio. No one had ever heard that he possessed any qualifications for Secretary of the Treasury, and he evinced none while in office, except blind prudence and personal integrity. He was an accident in the place, being there because it was necessary to put him somewhere; and, after doing no end of mis-

---

* Middle-aged men remember all this: it was a part of their personal experience.

† "That grandest statesman I have met in my fourteen years of Congressional life—old Thad. Stevens—was at the head of the Committee of Ways and Means. He had studied in all its bearings the question of French finance. He was familiar with Franklin's advice to the Continental Congress. The part he took in the debate exhibited, not only his marvellous powers, but his perfect familiarity with the history and details of the great and intricate subject."—*Wm. D. Kelley: Address by invitation of the citizens of Philadelphia, January 15th, 1876: Henry Carey Baird & Co., Publishers.*

chief with the best intentions, he retired into the Supreme Court, where he was competent and at home.*

When Lincoln's administration began, the federal treasury was empty; but, with the whole North committed to the Union, THE GOVERNMENT CREDIT became the CENTER AND SECURITY OF ALL PROPERTY. Without the government, what would be left to the Northern people, rich or poor? It was a time when Shylock himself was obliged to indorse his country's note, in order to save his own ducats. So the nation had the money-power at mercy—could perfectly establish its own fiscal solvency, and lay out any financial policy necessary to the general welfare.†

On the 17th of July, the Secretary of the Treasury was authorized to borrow two hundred and fifty millions of dollars, on bonds and treasury notes. The act left it at his option to issue fifty millions, in the treasury notes, of denominations not less than ten dollars, payable on demand, in coin, without interest. On the 5th of August, the restriction of denomination was changed to five dollars, and the notes were made receivable in payment of public dues. On the 12th of February, 1862, ten millions more of these notes were authorized, making sixty millions in all. On the 17th of March this issue was made receivable for "duties on imports," and was constituted "*lawful money and a legal tender.*"

These "old demand notes," as they were called, were the prototype of the "GREENBACK," AS CONTEMPLATED BY STEVENS AND SPAULDING, except that the greenback was to leave out the promise to pay "coin on demand," there being no possibility of fulfilling any such promise. But *here* was just the kind of money that had been advocated by Franklin, Jefferson, Adams, Madison, Jackson, Calhoun and Tyler, to supplement gold and silver. It was a GOVERNMENT NOTE, REDEEMABLE IN TAXES, and a CURRENCY FOR THE PEOPLE.

---

* "If Mr. Chase had ever been a banker or a merchant, he might have joined theory with practice, and had the aid of both; but, as it was, he only had the former—and that was a theory of his own brain, through his inordinate self-conceit, has cost the country, in all probability, a thousand millions of debt, beyond what would have been contracted on lower prices. I do not believe a more ignorant man, of practical business affairs, can be found in public life."—*J. S. Gibbons, author of "The Public Debt of the United States," contributor to Johnson's Cyclopædia, &c., in letter to E. G. Spaulding, April 6th, 1870, published in Spaulding's "Financial History of the War."*

† In this connection the "Muse of History" will never forget the words of Hon. William Kellogg of Illinois, in a speech to the House, on the 6th of February, 1862. It expressed the unanimous sentiment of the country, (except that of the Shylocks), as it stood in the summer of 1861. "I am pained," said Mr. Kellogg, "when I sit in my place in the House, and hear members talk about the sacredness of Capital. * * * They will vote six hundred thousand of the flower of the American youth for the Army, to be sacrificed, without a blush; but the great interests of capital, of currency, must not be touched. We have summoned the youth, and they have come. I would summon the capital. * * * Before this Republic shall go down I would take every cent from the treasury of the States, from the treasury of capitalists, from the treasury of individuals, and press it into the use of the Government. *What is capital worth without a Government?*"

But, to the "old State banks," the thought of such a currency was like holy water to the imps of Satan. Their own circulation had been a *monopoly*, on which the people had paid them *thousands of millions of dollars in interest*, to say nothing of spoils. The United States notes were a circulation on which the people *saved this interest for themselves*. The notes could be turned over to individuals, and corporations could bank on them, charging interest; but the government—that is, *the people as a whole*—had no "*shave*" to pay for the use of them. The bills of the State Banks, *when good*, had been secured by State bonds: in other words, the people were protected against loss in holding the bills, through the people's own dues to the States—State-taxes. But *Federal-taxes*, certainly, were quite as good security as State-taxes, and these Federal taxes were both the security and the direct redemption of the treasury notes.

BUT HIST! If such money as this should once become general—if the people should understand it, and should know that all the greatest "fathers of the Republic" had tried to secure it for them—*the banking-monopoly would expire.* Its inflated, interest-loaded currency, would be driven out of use, and those "old State Banks" would be relegated to the moral standing of the faro-bank—a much less vicious iniquity, all things considered!

So, the claw-fingered gentry of the "gold-basis" suddenly filled themselves up with spectacular patriotism. They had an interview with Mr. Chase. It was on the 9th of August, the banks of New York, Boston and Philadelphia being specially represented.* How they wanted to help the government! And how they sent out the report of their generosity through the newspapers! They agreed, with Mr. Chase, to take, at par, fifty millions of dollars in government paper, bearing seven and three-tenths per cent interest, with the privilege of a hundred millions more, and offer the loan to the people. They then proposed to Mr. Chase to *call in what demand notes he had issued*, to *issue no more*, and to *check out of bank their own bills*, to meet the government obligations. But Mr. Chase was not quite so impressible and uninformed as to walk into *so visible a trap as this*. He saw that the banks—those of New York, Boston, and Philadelphia together holding at that time only sixty-three millions of specie—would inflate their currency to the bulk of the war-debt, if permitted, and might then, if only through the necessities of their system, contract their loans and currency, and bankrupt both the government and the people, perhaps at the most critical moment of the war. Mr. Chase declined to gratify the noble souls of the bankers, to the extent of their sublime interest in skinning their country, and was slow to commit himself to any definite policy. He refused to receive their bank-bills for the loan they had taken, and insisted on specie. During the next four

* See Spaulding's "History of the Legal Tender Money issued during the great Rebellion."

months, accordingly, the banks of New York paid him eighty millions in coin. But nobody wanted to hold the cumbrous metal, and business was so active that the coin was returned to the banks about as fast as they paid it out. The immense calls of the government reduced their reserves *only seven millions of dollars.* There was nothing alarming, surely, in that reduction. But the bank-men were exceedingly discouraged by the obstinacy of Mr. Chase. As the soldiers and sailors of the Union needed money, he continued to issue those dreaded treasury-notes, which began to take the place of specie, to a considerable extent, in the reflux of currency to the banks. So the State-Bank patriots SUSPENDED SPECIE-PAYMENTS, and paid Mr. Chase, as far as possible, in his own issues, for the balance of their investment in his fund to save the Union. At first, they forced down the treasury-notes somewhat below par; for the Government had failed to make them receivable and payable for all public and private obligations—full legal-tender money.* The suspended bankers took what advantage they could of this state of things, to sell their *coin* at a premium. Then the Government evinced the purpose of making its issues good for all things that coin could pay for, in the United States. Thereat, as Thaddeus Stevens said, a little later, a "howl" went up from the "bankers and bullion-brokers," so "hideous," that nothing like it had been known since "their cousins," the money-changers of Jerusalem, were "kicked out of the temple."†

CHAPTER VIII.

SHYLOCK'S DEFEAT OF HONEST MONEY.

Of the regular session of Congress, which convened on the second of December, 1861, the most important Committee, that of Ways and Means, was made up with Thaddeus Stevens as Chairman. The committee appointed a sub-committee, its chairman being E. G. Spaulding. This gentleman, like Thaddeus Stevens himself, had probably no equal in the country for the task assigned to him. He was both a lawyer and a banker, and when the work finally *had to be done,* he drew up the National-Bank Act. He understood the uses and abuses of money, and has availed himself of both; but he was faithful to the people in the hour

---

* "This very thing," said Mr. Blake of Ohio, to the House of Representatives, on the 6th of February, 1862, "was done *here* only last month; soldiers were shaved by the money-shavers of this District from four to twenty per cent on the Demand Treasury Notes they had received from the Government."

† When the New York banks "suspended," their specie-reserves stood at not quite thirty millions of dollars. As they had discriminated against the government notes until made full legal-tender, the public naturally followed their example, and "hoarded" some of their cash.

of their greatest need, and for that fidelity they will never forget to be thankful.*

In 1861, Mr. Stevens and Mr. Spaulding tried, with all their might, to give us a system of money that would not slay our fathers and brothers from the rear, while they were saving our lives and property by fighting at the front.

In one sense, this system of money was not new. It was just *six hundred and ninety years old*. For not to mention the "lost arts" of Rome and Carthage, the first issue of the United States treasury-note of 1861 was essentially a copy of the old divisible inscription of the Bank of Venice. The difference was this: one was a government credit on the ledger of a nation's fiscal agency, and the other was a government credit in the hands of the nation itself—in the hands of anybody who had earned it. This money epitomized the whole worth of the Bank of Venice, supplemented by the only honest invention and real improvement ever due to the Bank of England, her circulating issues, if, indeed, these were not first due to the Bank of Genoa.† The plan, in fact, was so simple and sensible, upright and safe, that no other could have been conceived and adopted at the time, EXCEPT IN THE INTEREST OF CORRUPTION AND PLUNDER.

The Union was to be preserved, and the people were to pay the cost. Their agent, the government, was to make all disbursements, but ultimately the people themselves were to meet the expenses *in some form of taxation*. If a citizen, therefore, furnished any kind of property to the government, he was to be paid for it in government certificates of its value, good for all public dues. But such public dues were also the private debts of every citizen owning property—the unavoidable liabilities of the whole people. To no honest citizen, certainly, could anything be better money than these national certificates of value, received by all the people, for all the people, and payable for all claims against any one of the people.

It must be said, however, that Mr. Stevens, Mr. Spaulding, and their Congressional advisers, had no intention of being monetary philosophers or advanced economic reformers. They were simply a number of the most sensible and solid persons in America, of the usual sort—lawyers, bankers, merchants and manufacturers, especially familiar with business in every relation. It was no purpose of theirs to supplant gold and silver

---

* Hon. Elbridge Gerry Spaulding is now (March, 1894) supposed to be the richest citizen of Buffalo, N. Y. He is not reputed to be *benevolent*. The widow or the orphan would hardly expect to be saved by him from the profitable foreclosure of a mortgage. What may be his, *by law*, is not apt to be possessed by others. In regard to his own course during the Civil War, he sometimes appears to have grown rather flaccid, under the criticism of a banking class who never speak in behalf of their country, but always of themselves. Mr. Spaulding is not framed in the mould of a Stevens—is not a *hero;* but, in a great historical crisis, as a public man, he was *honest* and *just*. As men and things have turned out, that was much.

† Colwell says the Bank of Genoa *originated* the bank-note.

with paper money. They merely determined to place the boundless credit of their country at par with coin among American citizens, all alike. Their purpose—to repeat it specifically—was to put our national debt partly into the form of small circulating notes, without interest, FOR A CURRENCY, and partly into the form of INTEREST-BEARING BONDS payable "in coin," at the end of twenty years. The currency-notes were to be limited by law to a volume sufficient only to make them the absolutely needed vehicles of exchanging commodities. This limit would hold them at par. But, to make sure that the government should not be guilty of "inflation," *as the banks had always been*, the bonds were to be constantly on sale—an excellent investment in which any surplus of the circulating medium might be cut off and funded.

Mr. Stevens and Mr. Spaulding drew up their bill to give us HONEST MONEY. But, as soon as the bill was made public, the whole tribe of Shylock went into spasms. Every banker and broker in the land who had determined to prey upon the government and the people, saw that the whole swindle of *cornering production* with their special knave of clubs, called "the gold standard," was in danger of being suppressed, for *twenty years*, if not *forever*. For twenty years, at least, there would be never a "shave" in Wall-Street on a lump of bullion, and not one balloon of inflation to burst over a gold-pot. So a delegation of bankers and coin-venders hastened once again to Washington. They organized, and requested the Committee of Ways and Means of the House, and the Finance-Committee of the Senate, to meet them at the office of the Secretary of the Treasury. Their request was complied with, on the 11th of January, 1862.

They asked a few favors.

They asked for a direct tax, to the amount of a hundred and twenty-five millions of dollars—to shut off from the people, to that extent, a *tax-saving* money-volume.

They asked to have NO MORE "DEMAND NOTES" EMITTED by the government, but that an issue of a hundred million dollars be made, in treasury notes running *two years*, receivable for internal taxes, but non-receivable for *duties on imports*.

They asked that THE GOVERNMENT SHOULD DEPOSIT WITH THE BANKS —which *had all suspended specie-payments*—and should check out their depreciated paper-currency.

They asked that the Secretary of the Treasury *should negociate loans* with THEM, the modest money-power, as best he could, after an issue of money partially repudiated by the government issuing it.

They asked that, when the loans became due, he should renew them with government-bonds *at the market price*—that is, at any figure which large capitalists might have the assurance to demand.

This appears, according to Mr. Spaulding's account of it, to be about all that "the bankers and bullionists" asked of their troubled, imperiled country, at just that moment. But, within a month, they overcame all such insipid bashfulness, and asked substantially for "the earth," so far as it contained anything to prevent the government from conducting the war with integrity and economy.

For instance:—

They asked that United States notes—the people's only money to put down the Rebellion, carry on their business, and pay their debts—should not be invested with the right of legal-tender, and thus should not be made *money* at all.

They asked that it should be legally deprived of power to pay the bankers and bullionists themselves the interest on their own special investments in the nation's bonds.

They asked for the issue of two hundred millions of government notes, redeemable *in coin*, in *one year*.

They asked to have two hundred and fifty millions of bonds emitted for them, running thirty-one years at seven per cent, and that these bonds be exchanged for the bills of suspended banks in New York, Boston, and Philadelphia.

They asked that one hundred millions of United States notes, at three years and at seven and three-tenths per cent interest—which had been legalized on the 17th of July, 1861, and were *owned by the "Associated Banks"*—should be made LEGAL-TENDER; so as to displace a hundred millions of legitimate currency.

They asked that the Treasury Department should receive United States currency-notes on deposit, in rich men's aggregations of "not less than one hundred dollars," and pay five per cent interest on them; the main purpose being to avoid the necessity of putting the notes into bonds and aiding the government to re-issue its circulation.

They asked, also, that these United States currency-notes might be made convertible into the government issues bearing an interest of seven and three-tenths per cent, and due in somewhat more than *two years*. "Parties may buy these notes at a discount," said the great Chairman of the Committee of Ways and Means, "and put them into notes payable in bullion at two years, at seven and three-tenths interest—for that is a part of the whole system."

But enough. Shylock's delegation of bankers and brokers—really the most despicable of all traitors to their country in 1861 and 1862—were what their meek dupes have been taught to call "honorable gentlemen." They belonged to the "higher classes." It was very unfortunate they did. Had they been A DELEGATION OF BURGLARS, with "jimmies" sticking out of every pocket, they never could have had the demonic impudence to press their propositions. When their intrigues assumed form, and passed the Senate, as what Thaddeus Stevens termed "*the amended bill*" *of* "*the Associated Banks*," his blood boiled with righteous indignation.

"Was there ever" [he exclaimed] "a more convenient contrivance got up, into which blind mice run, to catch them! Was ever before such a machine got up for swindling the government, and making the fortunes of the gold-bullionists in one single year?"

It was simply a plot, by which the law-makers of the United States, instead of upholding the unlimited credit of the government, should be procured to *knock it down from forty to sixty per cent*, taking the vast difference out of the people, and turning it over to the delegation themselves, with the wealthy classes for whom they were scheming, but whose property the masses were *fighting and dying to sustain and save*.*

Those "gold-bullionists" were deplorably successful. It was not, however, that their purposes were misunderstood. THEIR WHOLE SCHEME WAS EXPLAINED AND EXPOSED on the instant. According to "The Financial History of the War,"

"The Sub-Committee of Ways and Means objected, through Mr. Spaulding, to any and every form of 'shinning' by government through Wall or State Street, to begin with; objected to the knocking down of government stocks *to seventy-five or sixty cents on the dollar*—the inevitable result of throwing a new and large loan on the market *without limitation as to price;* claimed for Treasury notes as much virtue of par value as the notes of banks which had suspended specie payments, but which yet circulated in the trade of the North; and flushed with firmly refusing to assent to any scheme which should permit a speculation of brokers, bankers and others, in the government securities, and *particularly any scheme which should* DOUBLE THE DEBT OF THE COUNTRY, AND DOUBLE THE EXPENSES, by damaging the credit of the government to the extent of sending it to 'shin' through the shaving shops of New York, Boston and Philadelphia."

Mr. Spaulding's great HONEST-MONEY BILL went before the House of Representatives undebauched by rascals. The House, of that term, was an assemblage of men fresh from the people, and distinguished by unusual patriotism, integrity and ability. Thaddeus Stevens made one of his most earnest and powerful speeches, to close the debate. He covered all objec-

* There were many and glorious exceptions to these bank-bandits. Stevens and Spaulding received letters from honest bankers, all over the country, repudiating the demands and the conduct of the dishonest ones. Mr. J. M. Ganson, one of Mr. Spaulding's fellow bank-presidents of Buffalo, wrote to him: "*Send home the Bank Committee: their proposition is* AWFUL. Let the demand notes assume the place of specie in *every* particular." The great Bank of Commerce, in New York, assured Mr. Spaulding that the "Committee" did not represent that institution, though the Cashier, Mr. Henry F. Vail, afterwards admitted to him: "You are correct in your supposition regarding my instrumentality in procuring the interest on bonds, &c., being made payable in coin." The Commercial forces of the country —Boards of Trade and Chambers of Commerce—demanded the greenback pure and simple— the same kind of money for everybody. Hon. Louis F. Allen summed up the general voice. "I trust," said he, in a letter to Mr. Spaulding, that "both Houses will put it" (the Legal-Tender Act) "right along through, regardless of what the New York note-shavers and usurers may say; for they and the like are the only ones who will oppose it, and that for the reason that they cannot make ten, twenty or fifty per cent, by buying in and selling out the *stocks* which they want passed by the Government, in place of the sound, available, *Constitutional currency* which you propose."—(See "Spaulding's History," &c.)

tions and all points. He was impressive, sarcastic, humorous, pathetic. In concluding his speech, he said:

"The Committee of Ways and Means have labored in the preparation of this measure to the best of their poor abilities. We are not infallible. We do not come near it. I am but poorly qualified for anything of this kind. But we have given it our most anxious consideration, and have consulted those whom we believed to be the best qualified to advise us. * * * So far as I am concerned, I shall be modest enough not to attempt any other scheme. * * * We believe that the credit of the country will be sustained by it, that under it all classes will be paid in money which all classes can use, and that it will confer no advantage on the capitalist over the poor laboring man. If this bill shall pass, I shall hail it as the most auspicious measure of this Congress; if it shall fail, the result will be more deplorable than any disaster which could befall us."

THE BILL PASSED THE HOUSE, by a vote of 93 to 59.

But the "gold-bugs" of that day had, for some time, given up all hope of coaxing, frightening, or corrupting the House of Representatives, and had applied their machinations exclusively to the SENATE. Of that assemblage, Mr. William A. Berkey, one of the most upright and useful annalists of our monetary legislation—and one who has specially gained the confidence of the "common people," has not hesitated to speak thus :*

"The Senate at that time was a small body, but twenty-four States being represented, with but three or four members whose ability rose above mediocrity. The occupants of seats once filled by statesmen, whose ability and eloquence had made the Senate of the United States famous throughout the world, they became puffed-up with ideas of self-importance which, with the venality of the Shermans of the body, rendered them easy prey for the sharks of Wall Street. * * * That the Senate was controlled in its action, in regard to the Legal-Tender bill, by improper influences, is not a matter of conjecture, but of history."†

On this point, in his Philadelphia speech of January 15th, 1876, Hon. William D. Kelley said, with a little more euphemism:

The bill went to the Senate, which is a small body, and unhappily is not always the most intelligent assemblage in the world; and, being very much pressed, is sometimes seduced by plausible arguments put forth by men of great respectability, such as bank-presidents and dealers in national securities.

* In his "Money Question," fourth edition, page 199.
† Mr. Berkey's reference, here, to John Sherman, is general—not specific as to *time*. On the 13th of February, 1862, Sherman made the strongest speech in the Senate in favor of legal-tender treasury-notes, and while he *voted* for the worst amendment to the House bill— "the exception clause"—he appears to have been willing to do anything needed to save his country in that perilous exigency. There is nothing to show that he had yet become a commodity. Again, in the Senate of that day there was one man, at least, who fully comprehended and frankly exploded the whole English banking-system. It was Senator Howe, of Wisconsin, who took exactly the position, on that subject, taken in this book. On the 12th of February, 1862, he said: "*All paper currencies have been, and ever will be,* IRREDEEMABLE. It is a pleasant fiction to call them redeemable; it is an agreeable fancy to think them so. I would not expose that fiction, only that the great emergency which is upon us seems to render it more than usually proper that *the nation should begin to speak the truth to itself; to have done with shams, and to deal with realities.*"

But let the record stand in the language of Thaddeus Stevens himself.* Referring to the passage of the bill in the House, he said:

"A doleful sound came up from the caverns of bullion-brokers and the saloons of the associated banks. Their cashiers and agents were soon on the ground, and persuaded the Senate, *with but little deliberation*, to MANGLE and DESTROY what it had cost the House *months* to digest, consider and pass."

In that hour of war, however, NO TIME WAS TO BE LOST. The bill had to go through, in *some shape;* for the UNION DEPENDED ON IT.

Judge Kelley told the story in this way:†

"I remember the grand old commoner, with his hat in his hand and his cane under his arm, when he returned to the House from the final conference, *shedding bitter tears* over the result. 'Yes,' said he, 'we have had to yield. The Senate was stubborn. We did not yield until we found that *the country must be lost or the banks be gratified; and we have sought to save the country in spite of the cupidity of its wealthiest citizens.*'"

On the 25th of February, 1862, THE LEGAL-TENDER ACT passed the Senate, for the last time, and became a law. But it was the law of the banks, of Wall Street, and of the "cousins of the Jews." The Senatorial servants, not of the people, but of this now gleeful crew of pirates, scuttling the ship of State, *had deprived United States currency of the power to pay interest on the United States bonded debt, making this special hoard of Shylock payable only in "coin."* As a consequence, it became necessary to make imports also payable in coin, in order to raise for Shylock his exceptional pound of flesh: and this was done, with fire in the eye and indignation on the lips, by Thaddeus Stevens himself.

"Without such provision," said he, [of coin-interest on bonds], "there would have been *no demand for a single dollar of gold* to be used in this country. * * * Being unable to defeat this provision, I procured to be inserted a provision making the duties on imports payable in gold. This was to enable the government to meet the payment of interest in coin. * * * These combined provisions form *a mine of wealth for brokers and bankers*. The duties and interest will require sixty millions of dollars in gold, annually, and soon double that amount. Now our banks and brokers have scarcely that amount on hand. *They may put the price as high as they please*—IT MUST BE PAID. * * * The gold would return to their vaults, possibly, by the payment of interest on THE VERY BONDS THEY HELD THEMSELVES, and so be ready for the same operation at the next semi-annual payment, DOUBLING THEIR CAPITAL IN THREE YEARS."‡

Mr. Spaulding—A BANKER, remember—and the most distinguished American banker of the time—the man who by reason of his special ability was assigned to draw up the Legal-Tender Act, and who is called

---

* His speech to the House, February 20th, 1862.

† In the address just mentioned—one of the ablest speeches of its kind ever made in America.

‡ Speech in the House of Representatives, December 19th, 1862.

"the father of the greenback"—was quite as severe in denouncing the miserable botch-work of the Senate as was Thaddeus Stevens himself.

"Mr. Chairman," said he,* "I desire especially to oppose the amendments of the Senate which require the interest on bonds and notes to be paid in coin. * * * I am opposed to all those amendments of the Senate which make unjust discriminations between the creditors of the government. A soldier or sailor who performs service in the army or navy is a creditor of the government. The man who sells food, clothing, and the material of war, for the use of the army and navy, is a creditor of the government. The capitalist is a creditor of the government. All are creditors of the government *on an equal footing.* * * * Why make this discrimination? Who asks to have one class of creditors placed on a better footing than another class? * * * Sir, it is a very respectable class of gentlemen, but a class of men who are *very sharp in all money transactions.* They are not generally among the producing classes—not among those who, by their labor and skill, make the wealth of the country. * * * The legal tender note bill is *a great measure of equality.* It proposes a currency for the people which is based upon the great faith of the people and all their taxable property. * * * The very discrimination proposed carries on its face notice to everybody, that although the notes are declared to be 'lawful money and a legal tender in payment of debts,' yet there is something of *a higher value * * * to pay a peculiar class of creditors * * ** —a kind of absurdity and self-stultification which does not appear well on the face of the bill. It is *an unjust discrimination* which *does not appear well now,* and *will not look well in history.* You will, if the Senate's amendment is adopted, *depreciate by your own acts your own bonds and notes,* and effectually destroy the symmetry and harmonious workings of the whole plan."

Samuel Hooper of Massachusetts—another member of the Committee of Ways and Means, and *another banker*—after stating that all the banks, with the whole business of the country, had suspended specie payments, the Government being obliged to do the same, said:

"The object of this Treasury-Note Bill is to furnish a substantial and uniform currency that will aid the Government, and enable it to receive its dues and make its payments, *like all others, with credits.* This bill declares that, for all dues to the Government and for all payments by the Government, these notes shall be received 'the same as coin.' One way to make them the same as coin would be to make them at all times convertible into coin. Another is *to use them, so far as possible, for all purposes for which coin is used;* and *in this latter mode their value will be the same as coin, unless the amount that is issued exceeds the amount needed for such uses.* * * *

"I am opposed to the amendment of the Senate which requires the interest of Government notes and bonds to be paid absolutely in coin, because its effect will be to depreciate these notes, as compared with coin, *by declaring them in advance to be so depreciated.* It creates a necessity for the Government to obtain a large amount of coin by purchase * * * which holds out an inducement to speculate on the necessity of the Government, by collecting and hoarding the coin against the time that it will be required by the Government to pay its interest."

In regard to another Senate amendment—the selling of Government bonds "at the market price," to get the very gold for which a needless demand was *created* to pay Shylock's exceptional interest—Mr. Hooper exclaimed:

* Speech in the House, February 19th, 1862.

"I consider the adoption of the fifteenth amendment of the Senate, which authorizes the Treasurer to sell the bonds at '*the market price*,' *as an invitation to the public to depreciate their value*, and so entirely contrary to the principles of the bill that I move to lay the bill, with the amendments, on the table."

Knowing that the bill would pass without his own aid, Mr. Hooper finally voted *against the Legal-Tender Act*, to show his abhorrence of the iniquities appended to it.

But that "small body," the Senate of 1862, gave no heed to Stevens, no heed to Spaulding and Hooper, no heed to its own few experts—no heed to anything but the pressure of the money-power, and as concentrated in the *very worst exponents* of it. At the beck of those who stayed at home from the war, and fattened on the gains of cheating the people and their defenders, William Pitt Fessenden, with his Senatorial infant-class in finance, outraged his country as cruelly, and much less courageously, than did Jefferson Davis and General Beauregard.* Three years and eight months later—on the 31st of October, 1865—the debt of the United States stood at nearly three thousand millions of dollars. Conceived in pillage and born in corruption, this debt had necessarily been nurtured in hypocrisy and chicane. So the Government scrip of indebtedness had been issued in a multitude of forms which nobody but gold-sharks and their lawyers had time to keep track of.† As for that part of the debt used more or less for a currency, it had been purposely created in such shapes that it could only achieve its purpose in a crippled and halting way. One half the volume, put out properly, would have done the work better than the whole nineteen hundred millions of it. The demand for gold, which the conclave of Shylock had induced the Government to *cause*, soon had its *effect*. Starting at par with coin in January, 1862, it took a dollar and thirty-seven cents of the United States Notes to buy a gold dollar, before the end of the *year*. Before the end of the *war*, it took, at one period, two hundred and eighty-five dollars, in soldier's, sailor's and the people's currency, to

---

* Mr. Fessenden, then Chairman of the Finance Committee of the Senate, was *honest*, perfectly so, it would seem, in the ordinary, conventional sense. He was simply a rather small man, a very good technical lawyer, and a person of prodigious gab, self-assertion and self-importance. Wendell Phillips used to criticise him as soured and minimized by dyspepsia. His sin against the American people was the sin of an *attorney*—accustomed to take *a case* and *do what his client wanted*. The money-power, vastly impressive to second-rate men, persuaded him, though doubtless without a retainer, to act in their behalf. His plea for them, as the record shows, was merely a string of their own sophistries, which *they* knew to be advanced implements for housebreaking, but which *he* knew not at all. He went so far with them as even to vote against *making the Treasury Note a legal-tender*, though Senator Wilson, one of the best business men of New England, assured him it was solely "a contest between brokers, jobbers and money-changers on the one side, and the people of the United States on the other." Every competent person knew well enough—as the distinguished Washington banker, Mr. Corcoran, afterward declared in a letter to Spaulding—that, without the legal-tender currency, "the War could not have been carried on six months longer."

† "I counted the different varieties of paper which were emitted untill, if my memory serves me right, the number reached *thirty-three*, when I gave up in despair."—*Letter of F. A. Conkling to E. G. Spaulding, Oct. 17th, 1875.*

pay for one hundred dollars in metal. Thus our bonds—our Government securities for the people's debt—were sold to the rich as low as thirty-five dollars on the hundred, to be paid at their full face, with high interest. The average difference between the greenback and the gold dollar shows the unnecessary and corrupt increase of the National Debt. We have seen that Mr. J. S. Gibbons, supposed to be an expert in the matter, has figured out the amount purloined by the bullion-corner at *not less* than a thousand millions of dollars, during the few years of the war only. Montgomery Blair, General Dix, and others, reached a similar amount of difference between a specie and a paper debt, though from an opposite point of view.* Judge Kelley said, in 1876:

"That crime perpetrated by the Senate of the United States has cost the American people more than all the war would have cost, had the House bill been adopted as originally passed. That crime or blunder called into existence the Gold-room of New York; it invited from all the money-centers of the world their most voracious vampires to come and fatten upon the life-blood of the American people. It converted commerce into a mere system of gambling, and made such creatures as Jay Gould and Jim Fisk possible in American history."

The exact figures are of no consequence. But when the shrewd yet honorable banker, Mr. Spaulding, acting as Chairman of the Sub-Committee of Ways and Means of the House of Representatives, indignantly protested that the demands of Wall Street and the Banks would "DOUBLE THE DEBT OF THE WAR," his estimate in advance was probably as near the truth as any that has been made since.

Those cormorants of the war-days occasionally buy, even yet, a eulogy of themselves from some newspaper, especially if there is anything in sight to steal. But Senator Voorhees once uttered a panegyric upon them which they never repeat. Of the American money-power he said:

"Not a patriotic act can be found in its history. It neither volunteered its services nor submitted to a draft. Its support of the government was purchased at the highest price ever paid by a bleeding people. It was in truth a traitor to the existence of the Union—a baser traitor than he who fought to destroy it on the field of battle. It hid itself from danger, and sold its assistance only for enormous pay, while the rebel soldier offered his life on the field of battle for nothing, except his devotion to an erroneous principle. While the soldiers of the North, too, were freely going to the front by the million, the capitalists, who now trample upon them and their children, were allured from their safe retreats, in the midst of their hoarded treasures, only by vast golden bribes. Neither in law nor in equity, neither in the sight of human courts, nor courts divine, have they any claim upon the forbearance or gratitude of the American people." †

---

* "I did not concur in the measure [the Legal-Tender Act] then, and still think it only aggravated the evils it was intended to meet, and added, as Gen. Dix estimates, at least $1,000,000,000 to our debt."—*Blair to Spaulding, Oct. 19th,* 1875: *Spaulding's History.*

† Quoted, with more like it, and with great fervor, by Berkey, in his "Money Question," (page 361), who calls Mr. Voorhees "the eloquent champion of the people's cause." How uncertain is the biography of a man before it is finished!

CHAPTER IX.

THE "NATIONAL" PROGENY OF THE "STATE" BANKS.

In his first annual report to Congress, Salmon P. Chase, as Secretary of the Treasury, recommended the establishment of the NATIONAL BANKING SYSTEM. A well-trained lawyer, he intimated, from ground with which he was familiar, that he considered STATE BANKS UNCONSTITUTIONAL. This may have been largely the reason for his dealing with them so gingerly. That he distrusted their agents, and dreaded their methods, his acts demonstrated. But those subtile-mannered men, with the prestige of millions, evidently impressed him with the need of their co-operation. In December of '62 he again recommended a National Banking Law, by which might be established " one sound, uniform circulation, of equal value throughout the country, upon the foundation of national credit combined with private capital." A perfectly honest man made this recommendation, intending it for his country's good, and not imagining that he would live to regret it.

The National-Bank bill became a law on the 25th of February, 1863. At that time, according even to the testimony of the man who drew up the act, there was no need of it whatever. Mr. Spaulding tells us * that

"No National-Bank currency was issued until about the 1st of January, 1864. After that time it was gradually issued. On the 1st of July, 1864, the sum of $25,825,695 had been issued ; and, on the 22d of April, 1865, shortly after the surrender of General Lee, the whole amount of Bank circulation, issued to that time, was only $146,027,975. It will therefore be seen that comparatively little direct aid was realized from this currency until after the close of the war. All the channels of circulation were well filled up with the greenback notes, compound-interest notes and certificates of indebtedness, to the amount of $700,000,000, before the National-Bank Act got fairly into operation. This Bank issue was in fact an additional *inflation of the currency*."

If, instead of a good politician and prudent attorney, *a great man*, like Thaddeus Stevens, had been Secretary of the Treasury, he would have known exactly what to do with the banks, and would have done it. Banks are useful institutions, and bankers are useful men. They are required as aids to business. Because a man is a banker, why should the Knights of Labor, for instance, formally exclude him from their order, as one who can in nowise be expected to be an upright citizen ? Banks and bankers have been a very important part of civilization. But they should not be permitted to ride and crush us with double interest, and with THE MONOPOLY OF ALL MONOPOLIES—the exclusive right to furnish and regulate the medium of our exchanges. In 1861 banking should have been made "free and equal," on the plan of all other things in America.

* "Financial History," &c., 2d Edition, page 188.

Rich men, or associations of men, should have been allowed to bank as much as they liked, on gold, silver, and the legal-tenders of the government, to discount commercial paper under proper safeguards, to charge interest on their loans, and to conduct all branches of their *legitimate* business. A statesman of first rate ability as Secretary of the Treasury, could easily have established such a system, in the early days of the Civil War. What, instead, was imposed upon our burdened backs?

Anybody who can see that one and one are not four—except under some scheme of larceny—can readily comprehend the National-Banking System.

A country is at war and has run in debt—to be paid some time, with interest. According to law, Mr. Shylockson, with four friends, buys a piece of this debt, represented by " bonds "—say of fifty thousand dollars. He has it locked up for him in a government safe, and lets it grow fat on six per cent. annual increase. The Government at the same time hands out to Mr. Shylockson forty-five thousand dollars printed for him in bank-notes—notes of " The First Shylockson National Bank." This institution is now set up. Mr. Shylockson lends to its customers, on discount, his forty-five thousand dollars, at such interest as the law allows—say from six to ten per cent. Thus, Mr. Shylockson, on an investment of *fifty thousand dollars* gets interest on *ninety-five thousand*. The interest on the forty-five thousand is paid by a few people around him; that on the fifty thousand, by *all* the people—the taxpayers.

It is quite right that Mr. Shylockson should have the interest on his *bond*, just so far as the issue of the bond has really been required ; but just so far as government paper is needed for *money*—for *currency*—just so far the interest-bearing bond should *never have been issued at all*, and the non-interest-bearing paper—say " greenbacks "—should have *taken its place*. The difference is a cheat—a " green-goods " swindle. In conducting this "business," Mr. Shylockson, president of the First Shylockson National Bank, is also a receiver of stolen property. Having been, too, a corruptionist at Washington, to legalize swindling, he has turned the United States into an accomplice—a thief procured to steal for his den. Moreover: if Shylockson had not gone to the Washington lobby as a political corruptionist, to get a monopoly, his country could have put out a currency sufficient for a *cash business*—such as the French do since they had a revolution, and guillotined the Shylocksons over there. Our Mr. Shylockson's bank-system, inherited from Hades and England, instead of Venice and France, is the only obstacle in America to what, in the main, might be a safe, honest, cash business. Then it would not be necessary for the people who happen to be Shylockson's neighbors, to depend wholly on him for money, paying him from six to ten per cent.—compounded three or four times a year—that very money being handed out to him from the people's treasury, *for nothing*, with the privilege of controlling its volume, and making it dear when he pleases. On the principle that he who has much should take more, the First Shylockson National Bank loans, in addition to its circulation, a certain average of its customers' deposits—drawing interest on what it owes, to pay for accommodating the public with what it steals. Though the big national banks have now become so greedy that they often eat the little ones, Mr. Shylockson's job is a good one—for *him*. But it is death to everybody else.

Some of the incidental workings of the National Banking System were glowingly described, in its early days, by Mr. S. S. Marshall, a member of Congress from Illinois, who gave this bit of history in the House:*

"An association of gentlemen in an Eastern State raised $300,000 in currency. They went to the office of the Register of the Treasury and exchanged their currency for $300,000 in six per cent. gold-bearing bonds. They then went to the office of the Comptroller of the Currency, in the same building, organized a National Bank, deposited their $300,000 in bonds, and received for their bank $270,000 in national currency. They had let the government have $30,000 in currency more than they received for banking purposes, and had on deposit $300,000, on which they received as interest from the government $18,000 a year, in gold, (and exempt from taxation). This was pretty good financeering, for these bankers to receive $18,000 a year in gold on the $30,000 in currency which they had thus loaned to the government. But this is not the whole story. They had their bank made a public depository. They soon discovered that there was scarcely ever less than $1,000,000 of government money deposited within their vaults. They did not like to see this vast sum lie idle. They, therefore, took $1,000,000 of this government money and bought $1,000,000 of five-twenty bonds with it. In other words they loaned $1,000,000 of the government's own money to the government, and deposited the bonds received in the vaults of their bank, on which they received from the same government $60,000 a year in gold as interest. Thus for the $30,000 in currency, which they originally loaned the government, they received annually in all $78,000."

Mr. Marshall's account of our National Banking has almost a touch of comedy in it. But when we remember that the STRUGGLING POOR AND THE PRODUCTIVE TAX-PAYERS have to settle for the larger part of such financial eccentricities, there is no great temptation to be merry.

The National Banks, as we have found, got under way in 1864—not until a year or more after the passage of the act creating them. There was a reason for it. Their stockholders and managers—not all, certainly, but the most alert among them—belonged to the *fraternity of the gold-bugs*. For three years they had exerted every human quality, except honor and decency, to injure the credit of their country, that they might speculate in her embarrassments. In 1864 they pushed up gold to an immense premium. Poor little Mr. Fessenden—their obedient servant of the Senate in 1861—who had now become Secretary of the Treasury, complained bitterly, and said they were "*very unpatriotic*," because they were taking full advantage of his own concessions to them. What a chuckle must

* July 21st, 1868: *Congressional Globe*; Appendix.

have been their answer! For more than a year, they kept gold at from fifty to a hundred and fifty per cent. above the government paper, of which they themselves had procured the depreciation, that they might buy it at the most depressed point. United States Bonds, at that time, fell to their lowest point, *thirty-five cents on the dollar*, for coin. Then the gold-bugs hauled in the bonds, and laid them down as the bottom of their National-Bank system, often doubling, by the trick, their whole capital. The people are trying to make up the difference, even to the present hour.

Those National Banks, as they themselves often claim, were very "helpful" to us. So they were. Their manipulators helped the rest of us at the very start, to get rid of all our property that *they* could lift and carry —and the end is not yet. But that which they desired most of all, and that to which they have bent every energy and accomplishment known to the Father of Lies, was to get away from the Government, and into their own hands, the ENTIRE CONTROL OF THE VOLUME OF MONEY. Give them the CIRCULATION and a GOLD-BASIS, and what shall keep any remainder of things out of their pockets?

CHAPTER X.

HUGH McCULLOCH'S DAY OF TRAMPS.

In 1865, immediately after the re-election of Lincoln to the Presidency, he appointed HUGH McCULLOCH, SECRETARY OF THE TREASURY. McCulloch was an unimportant banker, of Indiana, brought to Washington by Mr. Chase, and inherited by Mr. Lincoln from the office of Comptroller of the Currency.

From the ground we have now traversed, it is easy to see that the office of Secretary of the Treasury was then beset with extreme difficulties. Never had an outraged, war-worn people, more sadly needed a capacious head, an honest heart, and a firm hand, at their fiscal helm. On every side, for four years, they had been hampered and plundered; and now the shameless, pitiless spoilsmen who had overborne Stevens and Spaulding, had tortured Chase out of office, and hurried Fessenden on toward his tomb, demanded absolute control of the nation's coffers. In the distress of a heavily-laden, trustful soul, OUR MARTYRED LINCOLN TURNED TO McCULLOCH. Though of no public significance, there was one thing in favor of the Indiana banker: he had been far from Wall Street, while yet he might be supposed to know its ways, and how to cope with its chicanery.

McCulloch entered the President's Cabinet. But the pistol of an assassin soon took away from us our protector and friend, Abraham Lincoln. Then the man, McCulloch, disclosed himself. As Wilkes Booth murdered our beloved President, who was all fidelity to the masses, so Hugh McCulloch betrayed that fidelity, and wrung from his master's dead hand the blessings it held in store. The Western banker, brought East for a shield against the gold-thugs, handed himself over to the only foes of his country left within its borders, and became their cat's-paw of pillage and their besom of destruction. As Hon. William D. Kelley told the citizens of Philadelphia,

"Hugh McCulloch * * * hamstrung the whole nation. I affirm [said Mr. Kelley] that his management of the finances, while it *enriched him*, and made him a great London banker, has cost the American people *more than the war did*."

Berkey says:

"McCulloch not only entered into the designs of the money power, but became its most subservient tool, and retired with the reputation of being the first Secretary of the Treasury who had ever prostituted his high office for the purpose of enriching himself and his associates."*

To recount the deeds of this modern son of the ancient Moloch is to paint one of the blackest, most distressing and maddening pictures, in American history. And he made no mistake of pardonable ignorance. He knew precisely what he was doing.

"Henry C. Carey, who had a conversation with him immediately after his accession to office, says that he expressed himself then as unfavorable to contraction, and quotes him as saying that he 'should gladly see gold at one-seventy-five'—meaning that he would not favor contraction for the purpose of reducing the premium on gold. 'Three months later,' says Mr. Carey, 'he was instructing his representatives abroad to give assurances that we should have resumed specie payments before the seven-thirties became due.'" †

At the close of the Rebellion in 1865, the money-power, as we have seen, had nearly, if not fully, doubled the national debt. The armies of the North had disbanded, and our soldiers had gone to their homes. As well as they could, they had set to work, and there was plenty for them to do. The armies of the South had disbanded also, and the brave men in battered grey were doing their best to pick up some remnants of the old days. They had lost their cause, and were suffering the consequences of defeat— a disorganized and impoverished state of society. The North wished them well, and would have been glad to help them. It was the time to give every man in a re-united country the opportunity to put forth his best endeavors, that his country should heal and bloom, be fruitful and prosper. TO SUCH ENDS, MONEY WAS REQUIRED—a vast circulation of ready money. And of this there was enough, though not a dollar too much, for purposes so vast and beneficent.

But the bandits who owned Hugh McCulloch had other designs than these. Before the war, with no semblance of souls—nothing but pockets

*Money Question, page 218. †Berkey's "Money Question," page 218.

—they had mobbed the opponents of slavery, and had sneered at our American Declaration of Human Rights, as "a string of glittering generalities." When the war broke out, they had cringed in fear, and sneaked under the Union flag, that they might hold on to their gold. During the war, they had combined and conspired to make their country pay twice the normal value of the food and clothes, the guns and swords, by which it protected their lives and property. And now, with Hugh McCulloch for their national scoop, what was their further programme? IT WAS TO RUIN THE PROSPERITY OF THE NORTH, which her enormous industry had built up in spite of them. It was to enter her factories, her shops, her fields and homes, and to bid each and all of us "stand and deliver," in accordance with what we had. It was not to ruin the prosperity of the South; for that was gone. It was *to bind her fast*, and *tie her down for years*, to an incubus of penury and woe that might have been lifted and dispelled like a nightmare by the laugh of morning. It was to take from the maimed soldier of the Union, so far as possible, the money to buy his crutches, or his wooden leg. It was to burden his wife with harder tasks, and to withhold his children from school, that their little bodies might sweat for bread. It was to abet murder, to foster divorce, to multiply prostitution, and to impel suicide.

Well did the demons of Wall Street, of Lombard Street, and of the new and superfluous National Banks, with their "specie basis," do their work.

Their doings, even yet, have never got to the general public; for their hush-money has been bountiful, and their intimidations universal. But their method was simple. It was merely to play the old game of Ricardo and "Contraction," as played by the "gentle blood" and the Jews of England, in 1820, when they juggled the property of the island away from those who had produced it. It has been estimated that MORE THAN A MILLION men, women, and children were MURDERED—by starvation and otherwise—in this process of garroting the circulation of English money. When McCulloch followed the example of Ricardo, and made the people of the United States walk the plank of his craft of pirates, the result was about the same. Of many descriptions of this process, one of the most vivid has been given by Colonel Ingersoll:

"No man can imagine [said he], all the languages of the world cannot express, what the people of the United States suffered from 1873 to 1879. Men who considered themselves millionaires found that they were beggars; men living in palaces, supposing they had enough to give sunshine to the winter of their age, supposing they had enough to have all they loved in affluence and comfort, suddenly found that they were mendicants, with bonds, stocks, mortgages, all turned to ashes in their hands. The chimneys grew cold, the fires in the furnaces went out, the poor families were turned adrift, and the highways of the United States were crowded with tramps." *

* Speech on "Hard Times," by Robert G. Ingersoll.

After the historical facts we have now been over in these pages—facts standing in themselves for arguments—few readers, certainly, can have failed to grasp, by this time, the CHIEF LAW, and the CHIEF POWER, of money. No one ever made it clearer, by a single illustration, than Professor Bonamy Price, of the University of Oxford, in comparing units of money—dollars or pounds—with carts. His illustration has been touched in our "Introduction." Carts, wagons, trucks, are vehicles for transferring property from one person to another, and without such vehicles the property cannot be transferred. Money is also a vehicle for transfers of property, without which such transfers are impossible. If the supply of carts equals the demands of transfer, all sorts of goods are exchanged with facility at a fair price. If the supply of money equals the demands of transfer, the result is the same. But, *limit the supply* of carts or of money, and the price of their use "becomes high"—while the value of everything else falls in proportion to their scarcity. Hence, *nothing is more dangerous to industry*, and nothing is *more wicked, more disorganizing and deadly to society*, than a scheme which *abnormally contracts the volume of a people's money*. It should be set down as TREASON in the laws of every nation, and should be PUNISHED ACCORDINGLY.

In 1865, the legal tender money of the United States was, in round numbers, a thousand millions of dollars.* The population of the North was twenty-four millions. So there was an average distribution of forty-one dollars to each person, or "*per capita*." The return of the Southern States to the Union made a population of thirty-five millions, and a per-capita circulation of twenty-eight dollars. In addition to this currency of direct and full legal power, there was almost as much more, in amount, of short-time treasury notes, certificates of indebtedness and the like, which served to a considerable extent for money in large transactions. As a consequence, BUSINESS WAS DONE MOSTLY FOR CASH, and as McCulloch himself said, the people were *individually* "out of debt."

In December of 1865, in his first annual report as Secretary of the Treasury, this agent of the bankers and bullionists outlined their policy for them. The legal tender acts, he said, of the preceding four years, were "war-measures." Their character was temporary, and they "ought not to remain in force a day longer than would be necessary to enable the people to prepare for a return to the "constitutional currency"—this "constitutional currency" meaning the gold-piles in the corner of the syndicate behind him. He said that the retirement of Treasury Notes should be commenced without delay, and be continued until all should be retired.

---

*General A. J. Warner, in his "Facts About Silver," puts the exact amount at $985,000,000. At a time like the present, General Warner's little pamphlet, published by the American Bimetallic League, should be in every hand for reference. As authority for whatever it touches, there is absolutely nothing higher.

At the present day, it seems incredible that Congress could have been decoyed into approval of McCulloch's recommendations, and could have been so blind for two years, as not to check and snub him—which had to be done at the end of that time, but was done *too late*. We must recollect, however, that this pander to the Money-Power was hidden behind the massive form and the immortal shade of ABRAHAM LINCOLN. That a man supposed to be a friend of Lincoln, could stab his dead body by a scheme to raid his re-united country, few then imagined. In the excitement that followed his death, and the first measures of re-construction, with Andrew Johnson in his chair, almost nothing else received attention. As in 1861, so now again, the hard, soulless, ravenous gold-sharks, scented their prey and employed their pilot-fish. Congress meant well enough, perhaps, at the time, but was utterly opaque to the real purpose and end of Hugh McCulloch.

His duty was plain. No BANKER could have failed to see it, whoever else might be sightless. It was to save the people all the interest on their debt that could be carried in "legal tenders"; to pay the principal as fast as practicable in gold and silver "coin"; and to fund the rest of the debt, from time to time, in no way to prevent an increase of circulation, corresponding with increase of population and business. In accepting this sacred duty, there would have been enough benefaction, enough glory, for an angel. But, from the gold-bugs and the banks, there would have been *no money in it* FOR HUGH MCCULLOCH HIMSELF.

During his first year in office he retired forty-three millions of dollars in "greenbacks," and more than three hundred and fifty millions in other forms of indebtedness that entered more or less into the volume of money. By July 1868, he had cut the legal-tender and non-interest-bearing part of the national debt down to four hundred and six millions, having funded nearly all the rest in long-time bonds. In 1869, our money-circulation, including bank-issues, was less than seven hundred millions of dollars for forty millions of people.

Six years ago, speaking as a Senator of his country, Hon. Preston B. Plumb—the president of a national bank—declared that "*the contraction of the currency by* FIVE PER CENT OF ITS VOLUME means *the depreciation of the property of the country* THREE THOUSAND MILLIONS OF DOLLARS."*
Think of it; and, thinking, imagine the effect of the FIFTY PER CENT ✓CONTRACTION of Hugh McCulloch, Fra Diavolo, and their gang. Controlling, by their conspiracy, the people's money, all other property was sacrificed to them. From 1863 to '66, THE FAILURES IN BUSINESS, throughout the country, averaged something more than five hundred a year. The fiscal accomplishments of Hugh McCulloch raised the number, in due time, to nearly *ten thousand* a year. The list for 1873 was about fifty-two hundred, and, for 1876, ninety-one hundred.

* March 26th, 1888: see *Congressional Record*.

At the end of 1867, Benjamin F. Wade—a man of "the old school," who knew something about money—wrote to a correspondent:

"To talk of specie payments or a return to specie under present circumstances, is to talk like a fool. It would *destroy the country as effectually as a fire*, and any contraction of the currency at this time is about as bad."

Stout old "Ben" Wade was a little tardy in his cry. McCulloch's ravagers had already made sure of the "fire," and had arranged perfectly to "destroy the country."

A month later the pressure of public opinion forced Congress to muzzle and chain the Secretary of the Treasury, so far as to prevent him from any further retirement of legal-tender treasury notes—a special law being enacted for that purpose, which went into effect on the 4th of February, 1868. Some years later, Mr. J. A. Stevens, President of the New York Chamber of Commerce, explained the matter in this way:

"The country at large had felt the pressure of the screw, but had not been able to discover precisely from what quarter the pinch came, the contraction being confined to those outside forms of Treasury obligations which, though not currency in the strict acceptation of the word, were still used as such in the larger transactions of trade and financial exchange. When, in a time of general pressure, the currency itself became the subject of the pruning-knife, the country not only felt the knife, but saw how it was handled, and refused to submit to the 'heroic treatment.'"

What McCulloch would have done in the end, had he not been choked off, there is no knowing. HE MIGHT EASILY HAVE PLUNGED US INTO REVOLUTION. As it was, he shrouded us in misery, and sent out, on their dismal way, two millions of unemployed work-people. His hungry, houseless, helpless victims, were called "TRAMPS."

During the era of those "tramps," one great, kindly heart, at least—one eloquent tongue—one eminent and experienced statesman—told the *truth* about them. It was William D. Kelley, of Pennsylvania. Addressing his people, he said:

"You have seen a strong man, full of life, rise in the morning as a lion shakes the dew from his mane, and go forward to the battle of life, full of vigor, full of hope, full of energy, full of enterprise. * * * Bu. an accident happens; an artery is cut. The blood does not ooze, but flows from him. The surgeon comes just in time to save his life. He staunches the wound and binds it up. But the man is another being. He lies there pallid and shrunken. His sturdy limbs will not bear his wasted body. His muscles are flaccid, and his fingers have lost their skill. His energy is gone, and he dreams not of enterprise.

"This is our condition to-day as a people. In 1865 and 1866 every man in America who had the skill and the will to labor could earn wages to support his family and lay something by. All industries were quick and active. Production ran on. The American people waked up each new morning to feel there were great duties before them. There were mines to be opened, forges and furnaces to be erected. * * * New houses were built. * * * Our wealth grew as it, or that of any other people, had never grown.

"We were moving onward, *when one, Hugh McCulloch, tapped a great artery, and let nearly all the blood flow from the body politic.* Diseased, paralyzed, shrinking from day to day, what American has the energy to engage in developing a new mine? * * * Your laborers—moody, sullen, in want—are begging the poor privilege of earning a day's food by an honest day's labor. Their homes are being stripped of everything they cherish. Go through the suburbs of your city; halt before the houses where of a Sunday afternoon you would, a few years ago, have found the family gathered about the melodeon or the cheap piano, singing the praises of Him who had given them their lines in these pleasant places. Ah! the house is silent now; the father is out of employment, the sons are in idleness, the daughters have no work; the melodeon or piano is gone. Aye, worse than that, the most cherished mementoes, though of little value measured in dollars and cents—the cheap jewelry—the trinket that the young lover toiled in over-hours that he might buy and see it grace the person of his sweetheart—the amulet he hung upon the neck of his bride—the silver cup that marked the birth or christening of their first-born—cherished by all—but they have gone to the pawnbroker or jeweler to bring them food! Courage gone, hope gone, despair crushing him to the earth, and destroying all the pride that made the American mechanic the boast and honor of his country, *how many a man to-day, longing for honest work but powerless to obtain it, creeps and crawls from town to town, foot-sore, ragged, dusty, to beg from strangers rather than from those who know him and will remember it—to be denounced as a 'tramp,' and commended to the custody of the police!*"*

Mr. Kelley drew the sketch to the life in his pathetic address. And this handiwork of the devil was all for WHAT? That his imps, the money-power, might put THEIR price on OUR property—the property of honest brains, and skill, and labor. No words of indignation, no words of wrath, are adequate to the sins of such offenders. TO CLOAK THEIR DEPRAVITY, OR TO FORGIVE IT, IS ITSELF A CRIME. As they have scattered tortures and torments among mankind, so may tortures and torments fill their souls. With Tertullian and John Calvin, let us believe in a HELL! *It is needed!*

Hugh McCulloch, as report has it, still walks the earth—an old man of more than four score years, not worn out by remorse for deeds that have sent a million of his contemporaries to untimely graves! History, so far, has mostly walled up his career. For a long time his affairs have been largely abroad, with the British owners of national debts, and with the descendants of money-changers unhonored in Holy Writ. It would be well that the urn to his ashes should also rise abroad. If set up at home, the whitest marble will yet turn black in the shade of the public scowl.

* The Governor of one of our States—Mr. Lewelling of Kansas—was once a "*tramp.*" He said recently: "I know what it is myself to tramp the streets of a city seeking work and attempting in some way to earn an honest living. In 1865 I tramped up and down the streets of Chicago trying to get work. I was hungry, penniless, and was *subject to arrest*, but I was *not a criminal.* * * * *The economic conditions of the present are the trouble,* and men are *compelled* to wander around in search of work, not from choice, but from necessity." The brave Governor is right. Nine-tenths of all our "tramps" have been *made such* by men like Hugh McCulloch, John Sherman and Grover Cleveland. It is they, with their blatherskite-lackeys of the press, who ought to be spurned, whipped and arrested, instead of their helpless victims.

CHAPTER XI.
"SPECIE-RESUMPTION."

"Specie-resumption," as we know from our preceding chapter, was laid out, urged, and violently undertaken, by "one, Hugh McCulloch." *He* soon passed away from life in Washington, and went to the bosom of Dives, in Lombard Street, London. But in the course of time his twin-soul, if more subtile of brain, John Sherman, occupied his place as Secretary of the Treasury. THE SO-CALLED "HONORABLE" JOHN SHERMAN has occasionally taken a stand on the money-question in favor of the public welfare. When his fellow-citizens of Ohio have now and then roused themselves, and bristled with anger at the most impudent aggressions of his gold-fiends, he has deftly trimmed himself to the wind, and looked well that it might not blow him out of public office. In 1861 and '2, he appears to have meant well for his country. Was John Sherman really honest in those early days, or was the money-power economical of purchases that were not absolutely needed? Never mind. A few years later, he became the political attorney for every legislative abomination that Shylock could invent to rob the American people. However sad a thing it has been *for us*, we can readily conceive what a convenience it has been to the National Banks and the Bank of England, to have a chief-clerk in the United States Senate.

On the 14th of January, 1875, it was duly provided by law * that resumption of specie payments should take place in the United States four years subsequently—that is to say, commencing with the 1st of January, 1879. This law was of course an act of the banks and the gold-bugs. It provided for the unlimited issue of national-bank notes, which had been confined to a volume of three hundred and fifty-four millions—an arrangement to give the banks a complete monopoly of the nation's money. It provided that, as fast as the banks should put out their extra issues, the government legal-tenders—our "greenbacks"—should be "redeemed," to the extent of "eighty per centum of the sum of national-bank notes so issued"—a result necessitating the sale of bonds, and a perpetual load of interest for tax-payers on the investment. THIS BANKERS' STATUTE provided, finally, that all the "greenbacks," beyond those got rid of in this way—a balance of three hundred millions—should be "redeemed in coin, on and after the first day of January, 1879, on presentation at the office of the assistant treasurer of the United States in the City of New York, in sums of not less than fifty dollars."

The *purpose*, here, was the complete destruction of all the greenbacks. But, as the time approached, it was seen that, by *no human possibility*,

---
* U. S. Statutes: an Act to provide for the Resumption of Specie Payments.

could this intent of the law be carried out. The country neither *had*, nor *could procure*, gold for the purpose, and silver had been demonetized. As Senator Voorhees explained, in his speech of January 15th, 1878,

"The demonetization of silver was purposely accomplished before the policy of specie-resumption was declared, in order to make money as scarce as possible in reaching, by forced contraction, the single standard of gold."

So the Shylocks had overreached themselves, and they began to hear from it. To demand their pound of flesh would have produced a stringency of money, with a chaos of poverty, equal to that in France at the outbreak of her first revolution. The gold-bugs themselves might have risked even this "slough of despond." But Congress intervened, and, on the 31st of May, 1878, a law was passed, ANNULLING "RESUMPTION," so far as to require the RE-ISSUE OF THE TREASURY-NOTES, as taken up.

On January 1st, 1879, the United States Treasury had in hand A HUNDRED AND THIRTY-THREE MILLIONS of dollars IN COIN. There were THREE HUNDRED AND FORTY-SIX MILLIONS of "greenbacks" to be redeemed. What if these "greenbacks" had all been presented? The Government of the United States would have stood a bankrupt.

But John Sherman is a man who can see a point and meet an emergency—*till his time shall come!* How did he get coin? In 1879, John Sherman, Secretary of the Treasury, made United States treasury-notes exactly what Stevens and Spaulding had tried to make them in 1861—receivable for all treasury-purposes, including customs-duties and interest on the national debt. Then they turned into bank "reserves," and little was cared for the gold behind them. But this scheme threw the whole onus of actual specie payments on the *Government*, while the banks were left free to inflate the currency to any extent.

Thereupon, a personally harmless man, who happened to be President, and who did as he was told, prattled thus:

"I congratulate Congress on the successful execution of the resumption act. At the time fixed, and in the manner contemplated by law, United States notes began to be redeemed in coin. Since the 1st of January last they have been promptly redeemed on presentation; and in all business transactions, public and private, and in all parts of the country, they are received and paid out as the equivalent of coin. The demand upon the treasury for gold and silver in exchange for United States notes has been comparatively small, and the voluntary deposit of coin and bullion in exchange for notes has been very large. The excess of the precious metals deposited or exchanged for United States notes, over the amount of the United States notes redeemed, is about $40,000,000."

Rutherford Burchard Hayes was a pious and trustful soul. He was capable of faith even in John Sherman.

CHAPTER XII.

SHYLOCK'S MASTERPIECE—"THE CRIME OF 1873."

How silver was demonetized in the United States, in such a way that even the President who signed the bill* knew nothing about it for two years, was long a mystery. Of late, a good deal of nauseous courtesy has been wasted over it, among old party-hacks, in the Senate and elsewhere. But there is very little doubt that this deadly drain upon our life-blood— this vampire-suck at the daily sustenance of every man, woman and child in the land—was bought and paid for, like the ooze of a slaughter-house, by the Bank of England and the Jews of Frankfort. There is very little doubt that a retained financial adviser of European bankers, bondholders, and bullion-dealers, was sent from London to Washington, with half a million dollars in hand, and a million more at his back, to pay American politicians, who make our laws, to assassinate our interests. There is very little doubt that this smooth, able foreigner, succeeded in his work—that he found what he sought as readily as if he had been looking for pigs in a sty. There is very little doubt that WITH BRITISH GOLD—CHEAP FOR CASH—he procured an American betrayal of the American people as detestable as that of Calvary and the Cross.

Let us begin at the beginning of this plot—which the syndicate of Mammon who ride our Eastern press have forbidden their footmen to publish, but which, for the purpose of further suppression, now that the murder is partly out, these ink-pots of mendacity allude to, when they must, as "fictions of ancient history."

Thirty-two years ago, when the South rose in rebellion, and when the Shylock dragoons of the North shouldered their crowbars to break into the National Treasury, these fat soldiers of the jimmy and the dark-lantern not only *understood themselves*, but they were *perfectly understood by their like beyond the Atlantic*. So, in the autumn of 1862, a "confidential circular" was issued by an agent of European Capitalists to American bankers. The name of the agent was Hazard, and his Satanic production is known as

THE HAZARD CIRCULAR.

It was this:

> "Slavery is likely to be abolished by the war power, and chattel slavery destroyed. This, I and my European friends are in favor of, for slavery is but the owning of labor, and carries with it the care of the laborer; while *the European plan, led on by England,* IS CAPITAL'S CONTROL OF LABOR, BY CONTROLLING WAGES. THIS CAN BE DONE BY CONTROLLING THE MONEY. *The great debt that capitalists will see to it is made out of the war, must be used as a measure to control the volume of money.* To accomplish

---

* General Grant.

this the bonds must be used as a banking basis. We are now waiting to get the Secretary of the Treasury to make this recommendation to Congress. It will not do to allow the 'greenback,' as it is called, to circulate as money, any length of time, for we cannot control them. But we can control the bonds, and through them the bank issue."

There is no doubt of the perfect genuineness, and the diabolical good-faith, of this "confidential circular"; and, indeed, it need surprise no one who remembers, or knows through history, the general tone of the American moneyed-classes of 1860–'61 and '62. The circular was advisedly sent out, *in regular course of business*, to AMERICAN BANKERS. It was first made public by Hon. Isaac Sharp, at one time acting-governor of Kansas, and now a well-known resident of Washington. In connection with the Hazard Circular, Mr. Sharp published also the following

NATIONAL BANKERS' CIRCULAR.

"Dear Sir:—It is advisable to do all in your power to sustain such daily and weekly newspapers, *especially the agricultural and religious press*, AS WILL OPPOSE THE ISSUING OF GREENBACK PAPER MONEY, and that *you also withhold patronage or favors* FROM ALL WHO WILL NOT OPPOSE THE GOVERNMENT-ISSUE OF MONEY. Let the government issue the coin, and the banks issue the paper money of the country; for then we can better protect each other. To repeal the law creating national banks, or to restore to circulation the government-issue of money, will be to PROVIDE THE PEOPLE WITH MONEY, *and will, therefore*, SERIOUSLY AFFECT YOUR INDIVIDUAL PROFIT AS BANKERS AND LENDERS. See your Member of Congress at once, and engage him to support our interest THAT WE MAY CONTROL LEGISLATION."

This circular was signed by the official representative of the National Bankers Association, JAMES BUELL.

Mr. Sharp has explained his possession of the Hazard and Buell circulars in the subjoined letter:

"728 10th St. N. W., Washington, D. C., August 20th, 1890.

Col. Lee Crandall, Secretary of the National Executive Silver Committee:

Sir:—

"In reply to your polite request of yesterday, expressing a desire to be informed of the origin of the copy of the 'Hazard Circular' copied by the 'National View' some four years ago from the 'Council Grove Guard' then published by me in Council Grove, Kansas, I have to say that I obtained the original copy from a Mr. J. W. Simcock, the cashier of the First National Bank of Council Grove, Kansas. I, at that time—say about the year 1873—was the attorney for that Bank, and one day when the cashier was writing up and arranging a large number of accumulated letters and other papers of supposed value, either he or I came across the 'Hazard Circular,' together with the circular of the American Bankers and signed by one, Buell. I asked Mr. Simcock for these two circulars, and he gave them to me then; and, at the same time, in reply to questions I asked him, he said that their day of usefulness was over—that his friends in New York, some Bankers there, sent them to him, that he might the better understand the history and origin of the National Banking system, as he was comparatively a new Banker. I kept them for the light they threw upon the financial

questions of the times, and first published the 'Hazard Circular' September 18th, 1866, omitting the date therefrom, for the reason that it had dropped off—having been so folded that, when I came to print it, the date had lost off. The date was that of the summer or fall of 1862, but the exact month or day I cannot recollect—November, I think." "Very respectfully,
(Signed) "ISAAC SHARP."

As the writer of the present history, which I certainly mean shall be veracious, I must be permitted to say that I have the honor of personal acquaintance with both "Governor" Sharp and Colonel Crandall—the former a lawyer of distinction;* the latter a brave Confederate officer, in the old days, on the staff of "Stonewall" Jackson, but the first "Rebel" to decorate a Union Soldier's grave, and, for many years, a most enthusiastic editor in the service of honest money. I *know*, therefore, as well as any man can know a thing through another man, that the documents here given to the public, are genuine. I am personally informed by Mr. Sharp, that, some years ago, in connection with a brother frequently in Europe, occasion was taken to trace up the man, Hazard, then in London. He was at that time secretary, or solicitor, or both, of an English bankers' association in touch with bankers throughout Europe, and was financially connected with the Rothschilds. At last advices, he was still living. Mr. James Buell, who represented the *National* Bankers Association in 1873, became, in 1875, the founder and first president of the *American* Bankers Association. He was then President of the Importers and Traders National Bank, of New York City. He died about thirteen years ago, quite naturally a millionaire.

The Buell circular shows, by the BANKERS THEMSELVES, how deliberately they have subsidized the press, and have used Members of Congress to fit legislation to their special monopoly. But does anybody, in our day, need special proof on this point? As for the other document—the "Hazard" Circular—it is unique—a clear illustration of total depravity. But no man or demon ever knew better what he was talking about than this exponent of *the "European plan" of slavery, "led on by England."* Practical slavery, white or black, at any time or in any place, *can be instituted*, and *can be retained*, by any set of men who can CONTROL A PEOPLE'S MONEY. Mr. Hazard's philosophy of bonds and bank-issues is true also, beyond criticism. It was evidently written under inspiration—the plenary inspiration of the bottomless pit.

The Hazard circular, be it borne in mind, was issued as far back as 1862, just before Mr. Chase's second recommendation of our national organization of banks; and, considering the men of whom Hazard was the agent and representative, it is easy to see what vast though secretive pressure

* Mr. Sharp, when young, had the good fortune to be a favorite law-student of Thaddeus Stevens—the last one he instructed. This fact alone is sufficient to explain Mr. Sharp's interest in the Hazard and Buell literature, as soon as he saw it.

must have been brought to bear upon Mr. Chase, at that juncture, by the British banking-system of the whole world. He is said to have repented bitterly of the course into which he was honestly but weakly and mistakenly persuaded, and to have expressed his profound sorrow for it in these strong words:*

"My agency in procuring the passage of the National Bank act was the greatest financial mistake of my life. It has built up a monopoly that affects every interest in the country. It should be repealed. But before this can be accomplished the banks will be arrayed upon one side and the people upon the other, in a contest such as we have never seen in this country."

THE DEMONETIZATION OF AMERICAN SILVER, like so many other sins and misfortunes of our recent history, arose at first from our connection with European money-lenders, especially in England. They wanted less money in the world, so that their own special kind of property could command more than its honest value in everything else. They wanted *scarce and dear* GOLD for the principal and interest of their investments. When Hugh McCulloch was Secretary of the Treasury, Baron James Rothschild, with an English syndicate, owned United States Bonds known as "five-twenties," to the extent of four hundred and twenty millions of dollars, bought at about forty-two dollars on the hundred.† These bonds were payable in "greenbacks," explicitly, unquestionably, and as maintained, for years, by nearly every member of both houses of Congress who had anything to do with creating them, not excepting John Sherman.‡ Thad-

---

* This quotation has been "going the rounds of the press" for years. I have not directly verified it; but I have had in my possession a letter from Mr. J. W. Shuckers—Mr. Chase's private secretary and biographer—which states Mr. Chase's conviction that the people of the United States would yet thank him for bringing all the banks under a single head, that it might be cut off with one blow. Mr. Shucker's letter is in the hands of the American Bimetallic League.—G. C.

† I have the price, through a personal friend, from the European bankers themselves who purchased the bonds.

‡ On the 30th of March, 1868, John Sherman, from his seat in the Senate, wrote a letter which D. W. Voorhees reproduced on January 15th, 1878, in which Sherman said: "I think the bondholder violates his promise when he refuses to take the same kind of money he paid for the bonds. * * * He is a repudiator and extortioner to demand money more valuable than he gave."—"In less than ten months after this letter was written," said Senator Voorhees, * * * "John Sherman, then a Senator, advocated and procured the passage of the act of March, 1869, for the payment of the bonds in coin, which he had declared payable in currency, thereby establishing the open repudiation of a solemn and binding contract, and fastening an extortion of not less than five hundred millions of dollars on the staggering industries of the country as the speculative profits of the operation. In the whole financial history of the civilized world no parallel can be found to this audacious deed of broken faith, deliberate treachery to the people, and national dishonesty. * * * It will bear the names of those who enacted it to distant generations amidst the groans, the curses and the lamentations of those who toil on the land and on the sea; and, more deeply engraved than any other name, will be found that of the Secretary of the Treasury, [John Sherman] as the author of what he himself said constituted the twofold crime of repudiation and extortion."

deus Stevens—strongest of partizans that he was in all the Republican host—once said :

"If I knew that any party in this country would go for paying in coin that which is payable in money, thus enhancing it one-half—if I knew there was such a platform and such a determination on the part of any party, *I would vote on the other side*. I would vote for no such swindle upon the taxpayers of this country. I would vote for no such speculation in favor of the large bond-holders—the millionaires who took advantage of our folly in granting them *coin payment of interest.*"

God bless the upright soul of "Thad. Stevens." His memory shall yet shine like an August sun at noon, to blind and confound, to wither and destroy, the unparalleled scoundrels who have spent a generation in traducing him!

But, *for the time*, the dark-lantern and the short crowbar won the battle. From the end of 1862, or say from the passage of the National Bank Bill, to the end of 1865, *every act of financial legislation in the United States* was passed in the interest of the money-power, and for the purpose of bearing down the public credit. NOT ONE EXCEPTION CAN BE FOUND. But, when the war closed, "the criminal classes," who had done this work, changed face, and marched the other way. *Then*, all legislation was turned into the horns of a Wall Street bull, to toss up the value of bonds, and rip the taxpayer wholly to pieces.

By inducements adequate to the conscience of Hugh McCulloch, as Secretary of the Treasury from 1865 to 1869, he hastened to redeem in gold, or gold-equivalents, a hundred and fifty millions of Baron Rothschild's bonds, payable in *paper* until the end of twenty years. It was doubtless a great accommodation to that impecunious Hebrew, which must have been appreciated; for the redemption went on, in the same way, until his batch of five-twenties, with the rest of the issue—FIVE HUNDRED MILLIONS IN ALL—were out of the way. The transaction has been figured out, very briefly, thus:

```
Amount of the bonds ................................$500,000,000
Coin-interest, semi-annually, for ten years.............. 408,096,133
                                                        $908,096,133
Bond-holders' cost, at 42 cents on the dollar .............. 210,000,000
    Profit in ten years...........................$698,096,133
```

And this "deal" of seven hundred millions is only *one example* of the general manner in which the American people have been treated in the settlement of their National Debt. What a fragrant bouquet should Baron Rothschild have presented to Hugh McCulloch!

But the most direful part of this business between Rothschild and the United States Treasury, was not the *loss of money*, even by hundreds of millions. It was the resignation of the country itself INTO THE HANDS

OF ENGLAND, as England had long been resigned into the hands of HER JEWS. In 1868, Rothschild's American agent, August Belmont, turned up as Chairman of the Democratic National Committee, that the Anglo-Jew octopus, which had seized the Republican Party, might seize the Democratic Party also. That was before the advent of Grover Cleveland, and the Democratic Party rebelled. For the approaching election, it put into its platform an anti-Rothschild plank:

"Resolved: When the obligations of the government do not expressly state upon their face, or the law under which they were issued does not provide that they shall be paid in coin, they ought in right to be paid in the lawful money of the United States."

This plank settled the fate of the Democrats. Belmont had purchased a large interest in the leading Democratic newspaper—the New York "World." Just before election, he turned over this interest to Manton Marble, with the understanding that the "World" should denounce its own candidate, the venerable Horatio Seymour, as unfit for the Presidency, and should demand his "withdrawal"—a course which naturally disorganized and completely routed even his most determined followers. Here was the monstrous old taint of treachery in the blood, as in the days of Christ; but Democratic candidates have since been more obedient, and most Republican candidates have been the very tentacles of the octopus itself.

From 1868, we now look back one year—to the INTERNATIONAL CONFERENCE OF PARIS, in 1867. Mr. Samuel B. Ruggles, a member of the New York Chamber of Commerce, and a pioneer of the gold-plot, had procured the appointment of delegate from the United States to that Conference. John Sherman, of Ohio, was Chairman of the Committee on Finance in our National Senate. In May of 1867, Mr. Sherman was cultivating his taste for money and the other fine arts, as a tourist in Europe. The public significance of his tour has been explained by Senator Stewart:*

"After the close of the Russian-Turkish, the Prussian-Austrian, and our great war [says Mr. Stewart], speculation in the debts growing out of those wars centered in London. In 1867, Mr. Sherman * * * visited that city. After spending some time in London, where he had the opportunity of consulting the manipulators of bonds, he appeared in Paris, where a conference of nations was assembled to consider the unification of coins, weights and measures."

The International Conference of 1867 was held at the invitation of Louis Napoleon, the French Emperor, for the purpose of extending the principles of the Latin Union formed in 1865, through which France, Italy, Greece, Belgium, and Switzerland, agreed on common coins. But "the establishment of the SINGLE STANDARD, EXCLUSIVELY OF GOLD,"

* In the "Arena" of August, 1893.

was "the cardinal, if not the all-important feature of the plan proposed by the Conference."* Of this single gold-standard JOHN SHERMAN stood the most pronounced advocate.

On the 17th of May, 1867, Mr. Sherman being in Paris, conveniently near his friend and co-worker, Mr. Samuel B. Ruggles, Mr. Ruggles advised Mr. Sherman, by letter, that the International Conference was then in session, "*to agree if possible, on a common unit of money.*" Mr. Ruggles further advised Mr. Sherman that the proposition of the Conference was to take, for that common unit, the French five-franc gold-piece. The next day—May 18th—Mr. Sherman replied to Mr. Ruggles, favoring the proposition. He said:

"If this is done, France will surely abandon the *impossible effort* of making *two standards of value*. Gold coins will answer all the purposes of Europe."

Mr. Sherman's views were thereupon communicated to the Conference, as those of the Chairman of the Committee on Finance of the United States Senate.

Where Mr. John Sherman got such views, it is easy to perceive. For the first time in the world, they had just become current in London and New York, though only among men like Mr. Hazard and his banking forces, who contemplated "a new form of slavery" for mankind, "led on by England." Mr. Sherman's "impossible effort" of "making two standards of value," if he meant the joint standard of gold and silver, had *been* made in France, with perfect definiteness, since 1803; and Mr. Sherman's own country had never made any other standard than what he called a "double" one for more than three hundred years of that country's history. It has been said that Mr. John Sherman, in the year 1867, must have been "imbued with the mischievous idea" that gold possessed "*intrinsic*" value, "which made it a fixed standard for the world." This charitable theory, indeed, was expressed by so high an authority as General A. J. Warner, Chairman of the National Executive Silver Committee, as late as 1890. A full analysis, however, of Mr. Sherman's speeches, conduct and character, will permit no one to believe that he, of all men in America, has ever been so embryonic, since he emerged into public life, as not to know, at least, with the Hebrew prophet, Ricardo, that the value of money, like everything else, depends simply on the law of supply and demand. In 1861 and 1862, when John Sherman was poor and upright, he stood pretty well for honest money, and showed that he had comparatively a large grasp of the question. As late as February of 1867, he strongly favored, (for appearances and place at least), the payment of United States bonds in greenbacks—"the same kind of money," he said, "of the same intrinsic value it bore at the time they were issued."† In

---

* Official report by Ruggles, Nov. 7th, 1867.   † Speech, Feb. 27th, 1867.

1869, he clearly explained the terrors of monetary contraction, then well under way, and termed it "an act of folly without an example of evil in modern times.". On June 9th, 1868, in the very act of urging in the Senate "a single standard exclusively of gold," he spoke of gold as a "*commodity*," varying in value "*like other commodities*"—thus inadvertently showing "the intrinsic value of gold" to be a variable and relative value, and otherwise a myth, to *him*, however he might wish to impose it upon others as a reality. The great trouble, indeed, with John Sherman, lies in what is now the evident fact that he knew the principles of money only too well, at a time when they had been overslaughed and forgotten in the United States, except among the tools and disciples of Mr. Hazard. What, then, was the Ohio Senator doing in Paris twenty-seven years ago, just after his visit to London? From better circumstantial evidence than that on which many a man has been hanged, the conclusion is here drawn that the so-called "honorable" John Sherman was then abroad looking for a job which he ultimately secured, and which he finished up in 1873. In short, it has become clear enough that in the days of the Paris Conference there was a financial undertow in the affairs of men, which would have been very apt to land a political attorney of the National Bankers on the Continent of Europe. Nine years later a remarkable letter purporting to come from Paris—that beautiful city which had received the felicity of Mr. Sherman's visit— revealed reasons enough for his pilgrimage. The letter appeared on the 18th of May, 1876, in the "New York Daily Graphic," as subjoined:

A GIGANTIC OPERATION.

THE CAPITALISTS DOUBLING THEIR WEALTH BY DEMONETIZING SILVER.

A CURIOUS LETTER FROM A FRENCHMAN—SCHEMES BY WHICH SILVER WAS DEMONETIZED.

PARIS, May 6.—I have recently been in the employ of one of the leading banking houses of the world, and I think it due to the American public that they should be made acquainted with one of the most tremendous financial operations ever known in the history of mankind. I was trained early in life for a financial career, and I learned to write and speak fluently German, French, English and Dutch.

In my confidential relations with the various great banking houses—as correspondent for a leading firm—and by means of a stray letter which came accidentally into my possession, I acquired information that seems to me of the very highest importance. As FAR BACK AS 1863, *letters were received by the Rothschilds in this city pointing out the evil effects which were likely to follow from the use of paper money in America*. Prices were then rising in your country, and I judge bankers were puzzled to know what to do with your American securities and evidences of debt.

The adoption of the "legal tender act," as you call it in your country, made it possible to pay, in depreciated paper, debts contracted in coin. Much correspondence ensued among the European bankers touching American affairs, and it led to a determination which, however, was not finally reached until towards the close of the Franco-German war. *This determination was for a plan of bringing the power of all the great* bankers of the world upon the governments of the world to substitute the gold basis for all commercial transactions in place of the silver basis or the mixed basis of gold and silver.

WHENEVER THERE IS A SCARCITY OF COIN IT HAS INURED TO THE BENEFIT OF THE CREDITOR CLASS. PRICES HAVE RULED LOW, AND A SMALL SUM WOULD PURCHASE A GOOD DEAL OF RAW OR MANUFACTURED MATERIAL.

But the intercourse between nations, the invention of paper money, of bills of exchange, of bank currency and credit—in fact, all the saving devices of modern commerce—tended to make money plenty and prices high. Everything in that position of affairs worked against the creditor class and in favor of the debtor class.

This, it will be seen, was *a beneficial tendency for the masses of the people*. It compelled capitalists to increase their efforts in order to maintain their position. *It favored the debtors, who are always the enterprising part of the community.*

The man who does not go in debt is the speculator: he lends and absorbs, but does not start new enterprises, nor does he add to the wealth of the community. The consequence of this is that the cheapening of money is good for all business, and benefits a very large class of the community.

The great money-lenders of Europe (as the letters which passed under my inspection clearly proved) determined to reverse this tide in affairs, this general cheapening of money, which has been going on for 300 years. I HAVE INDISPUTABLE EVIDENCE IN MY POSSESSION THAT AN IMMENSE FUND WAS RAISED TO BRING ABOUT THE GENERAL ADOPTION OF THE GOLD-METAL BASIS.

The money writers and political economists in London, Paris, Berlin, Frankfort and Amsterdam were either argued into the adoption of these views or were *purchased outright*. HENCE THE ARTICLES IN THE LEADING PAPERS IN EUROPE IN FAVOR OF THE GOLD BASIS IN PREFERENCE TO THE SILVER OR THE MIXED BASIS.

Of course, the object of the great capitalists of Europe is quite apparent in the crusade against silver. BY REDUCING THE CURRENCY ONE-HALF IT WOULD ADD ENORMOUSLY TO THEIR WEALTH BY CHEAPENING PRODUCTS AND GIVING THEM A STILL GREATER MONOPOLY OF THE CIRCULATING MEDIUM. If the records could be searched it would be found that the demonetization of silver in England, Germany and Holland and its practical demonetization in France, was effected simultaneously with the passage of the gold act by the American Congress—I think that was in 1873—getting rid of the old silver dollar, the unit of value on which your debt was contracted.

In other words, the great capitalists of the world, by a gigantic conspiracy, like the Roman emperors of old, managed to tax the whole civilized world from ten to twenty per cent for their own personal benefit. The object was to make the very rich richer and the very poor poorer. With silver demonetized, gold would of course appreciate considerably in value, and all who were creditors to governments or for individual debts would have their evidences of debts greatly enhanced in value. Gold is the currency of the rich; silver, throughout the civilized and uncivilized world, is the money of the great mass of the community.

The small retail traffic of life is all managed by means of silver. By getting rid of silver these rich bankers and capitalists added billions of thalers to their possessions. IF THE FACTS COULD EVER BE BROUGHT TO LIGHT IT WOULD BE FOUND THAT THE AMERICAN CONGRESS WAS BRIBED BY THE CAPITALISTS OF EUROPE AND THIS COUNTRY TO GET RID OF THE SILVER DOLLAR AND SUBSTITUTE GOLD.

That corruption was employed in Germany is open to doubt. Bismarck could not be prevailed upon to make the change from silver to gold until he became alarmed at the demoralization caused by the payment of the French indemnity. The vast masses of gold thrown upon Germany by the payment of the French tribute raised prices, checked production and stimulated feverish speculation. Thereupon Bismarck was induced to try to utilize the gold by expelling silver.

In small countries like Holland the matter could be easily managed. The movement succeeded in England, although it was apprehended that it would destroy the commerce of India, which is carried on exclusively on a silver basis; and this fear was well founded. But the "Economist" and other financial papers in London support this gigantic conspiracy of the capitalists.

You may ask why do I, a confidential agent, tell of this? Because, frankly, I think the facts ought to be known to the world. Then I am a Red Republican in my heart. I believe in the solidarity of the people—in fraternity—in the splendid future in which Europe will be one great Republic. It seems to me that the cry should be raised by the laboring classes for a repudiation of all the national debts of the world. The capitalists have shown themselves so tyrannical, so antagonistic to the interests of the masses of the community, that no mercy should be shown to them. They have by their recent action in the demonetization of silver added most unjustly to the debts of all nations. And the same want of conscience which they have shown to the community should be manifested towards them in kind. But, alas, the working people are without leaders. There is no means of making them understand *this very simple matter*. But surely the American people ought to know the exact facts in this case, and should apply the remedy if it is possible to do so.

RUE ST. HONORE, PARIS.   HIPPOLYTE GRENIER.

In dealing with this extraordinary letter, it must be said at once, that, as far as the specific *nominal source* of it is concerned, it has been questioned by impartial authority, no less a person than Hon. Alexander Del Mar being the chief instance. Mr. Del Mar points to the fact that the substance of the letter had been largely anticipated in a Senatorial address by Mr. Jones, of Nevada, on the 24th of April—about a month before the letter appeared in the "Graphic." The English of the Paris correspondent is observed to be not only correct, but technical—too idiomatic for a foreigner —and he makes at least one noticeable mistake, that of including England among countries which had *recently* demonetized silver. On the other hand, a Frenchman's English would be well cared for before reaching the type of a New York journal; and the letter as a whole, while it might have been written by a well-informed bank-clerk, is not the work of a trained writer on monetary economics. Mr. James Croly, the editor of the "Graphic" in 1876, gave prominent editorial notice to the letter, and referred to it, distinctly, as coming "from Paris." Mr. Croly's associates regarded it as genuine,* though the name, "Hippolyte Grenier" might not have been the actual name of the writer. But all these "pros and cons" are really of no consequence. *Somebody* had got hold of a lot or FACTS, which were vital to the public, and the "Graphic" published them. But, from that day, the "Graphic" declined. It was too ingenuous, too babbling. Government contracts were withheld, bank patronage was withdrawn, and the paper, I am told, was "as good as ruined."

* So I learn from Colonel Lee Crandall, who was one of them.

In connection with Monsieur Grenier, whoever he was, let us now pause only one instant, and ask one question. *He*, at least, considered the understanding of money "*a very simple matter*," and proved it in a most practical way. But are we to suppose that John Sherman—our Senatorial expert of finance—a man in constant relation, on two hemispheres, with the principals for whom Monsieur Grenier described himself as a "clerk"— could have known less about this whole bad business, in 1873, than some "Graphic" correspondent knew in 1876? Oh, for the imagination of a Rider Haggard, to find one honest hair in the head of John Sherman!

On the 28th of April, 1870, THIS MAN introduced, in the Senate, the bill which, two years and ten months later, deprived the American people of about one-half their power to conduct their affairs and to pay their debts, and increased, in proportion, the assets of foreigners, misers, gamblers, and usurers. The bill was entitled

"AN ACT REVISING AND AMENDING THE LAWS RELATIVE TO THE MINTS, ASSAY-OFFICES, AND COINAGE OF THE UNITED STATES."

The real purpose of "The Mint Bill" being to demonetize silver, the thing was of course a fraud, even by name. Conceive the attempt to change the whole nature and effect of a people's money for more than three centuries, and the world's money for four thousand years—to take from one-half of this money its debt-paying function from time immemorial— under the mask of regulating the duties and stipends of metal-servants, puddlers and tinkers, branch-mints, emblems and clippings!

But soon after his trip to London and Paris, John Sherman had *tested* an open, straightforward attempt to establish "a single gold standard," and had *failed* at the very first step. On the 6th of January, 1868, he introduced, in the Senate, "A BILL IN RELATION TO THE COINAGE OF GOLD AND SILVER," which was referred to his Committee on Finance, and which he brought up on the 9th of June, urging it strongly, on the ground of the reports by Ruggles of the proceedings of the Paris Conference. The chief proposition of this bill, as summarized by Mr. Sherman, was "A SINGLE STANDARD EXCLUSIVELY OF GOLD."* Appealing to what he evidently considered might be a good deal of patriotic vanity in his fellow Senators, he said, "*the single standard of gold is an American idea*, yielded reluctantly, [at the Paris Conference], by France and other countries, where silver is the chief standard of value." The ostensible purpose of the Sherman plea, as a whole, was "the great object of unification of coinage."

Few Americans, we remember, in 1868, knew anything about money, apart from the getting of it. Mr. Sherman was a notable exception. He

---

* See Congressional Record under dates given, or speech by Senator Wm. M. Stewart, Sept. 5th, 1893, containing the full account of these proceedings.

had grasped the great law of volume in currency, and had manifestly determined to learn, at any moral sacrifice, the practical point of acquisition. With him, on the Senate's Committee of Finance, there happened to be another man—and an *honest* one—who also understood something of monetary principles. It was the great merchant and "war-governor" of New York, Senator E. D. Morgan. Mr. Morgan appears to have seen pretty well through the Sherman scheme, and he put his foot on it instantly. He submitted a minority report, in which he opposed "international regulation" of money as something that would "fetter ourselves," and pronounced the coinage of the United States "*the simplest of any in circulation.*" Of the silver dollar, he said we should "*do well to increase rather than discontinue its coinage,*" and he showed that the "two streams of the precious metals" should "be poured into the current of commerce in full volume." Mr. Morgan said further:

"The war gave us self-assertion of character, and removed many impediments to progress. * * * Its expensive lesson will be measurably lost if it fails to impress upon us the fact that *we have a distinctive American policy to work out—one sufficiently free from the traditions of Europe to be suited to our peculiar situation and the genius of our enterprising countrymen.*"

The end of Mr. John Sherman's FIRST ATTEMPT to demonetize silver was this:

"The bill *was never called up for action*. If it had been, the reading of Mr. Morgan's report would have settled its fate, and it would not have received a single vote in the Senate. * * * Neither the bill nor the report attracted the slightest attention, and it is doubtful if any Senator who was not on the Finance Committee ever knew that such a bill had been introduced. * * * But the report of Mr. Morgan must have satisfied the promoters of the scheme to demonetize silver, that a discussion in the Senate would be fatal to the object of their desire. * * * *He* had full knowledge of the objects of the bill, which he *defeated;* but the Senate and the country were ignorant of the whole transaction. * * * *No discussion in either House had taken place,* * * * *and Senators are too busy to examine the reports of committees upon bills which are never called up for action.*"*

The "War-Governor of New York"—a true American—having extinguished the Sherman gold-bill of 1868, as introduced in the Senate *undisguised*, nothing was left for Shylock's cook but to skulk behind some

---

*Citation from speech of Senator Wm. M. Stewart, of Nevada, Sept. 5th, 1893. In addition to this speech, Mr. Stewart has made two others within three years, virtually on the same subject—one of June 5th, 1890, and the other of June 1st and 2d, 1892. The three speeches together cover the entire history of the demonetization of silver in the United States, and the so-called "honorable" John Sherman will never find escape from them. They convert his whole character into an ash-heap. The invincible Senator of Nevada has insisted on putting all the facts on record, though they have frequently exhausted the British Wall-Street Senators so grievously that they could only keep alive by going out to drink, leaving the Senate without a quorum. Senator Stewart has served his constituents faithfully, and his country superbly.

"Mint Bill," and mix up his poison with the night-spoon of a conspirator. So, on the 28th of April, 1870, John Sherman introduced his anomalous measure which demonetized silver.

The latest account of this transaction, as given by himself, is contained in a speech to the Senate on the 30th of August, 1893.* In that speech he says:

"I now wish to call attention of the Senate to * * * the act of 1873, which has been the subject of so much *misrepresentation* and *falsehood*. I propose * * * to show, in the most unequivocal manner, the deception and falsehood, largely the result of *cowardice*, that has been uttered in respect to the act I refer to."

Again Mr. Sherman says:

"Sir, I would rather stand this day before you *defending a law which has been denounced and vilified*, as this has been, boldly avowing that *I did read the law* and that I *knew its contents*, than to plead the *baby act*, and say I did not know what was pending here before us for two or three years as an act of legislation."

Very well. But everybody knows, and the file of every American newspaper proves, that the PEOPLE of this country, at least, knew nothing in regard to the demonetization of silver until 1876, or about the time the New York "Graphic" published the letter signed "Hippolyte Grenier." On the 6th of March of that year, Mr. Bogy of Missouri summarized the matter in the Senate.†

"Our coinage act, [said he], came into operation on the 1st of April, 1873, and constituted the gold one-dollar piece the sole unit of value, while it restricted the legal tender of the new silver trade dollar and the half-dollar and subdivisions to an amount not exceeding $5 in one payment. Thus the double standard previously existing was finally abolished, and the United States, as usual, WAS INFLUENCED BY GREAT BRITAIN in making gold-coin the only standard. THIS SUITS ENGLAND, BUT DOES NOT SUIT US."

* It is entitled "The Purchase of Silver Bullion," and begins on page 915 of the "Congressional Record," date of August 31st.

† Senator Bogy's speech was made in support of a petition from the New York Chamber of Commerce against the resumption of specie payments, which that innocent body of merchants, and the like, supposed was to be a literal *coin* resumption, with *nothing to meet it*. They were not aware, at that time, that John Sherman had the gift of miracles, and could turn three hundred and fifty millions of *greenbacks* into *gold*. The chameleon-necromancer, Sherman himself, had said in 1869: "It is not possible to take this voyage [resumption] without the sorest distress. To every person except a capitalist out of debt, or a salaried officer or annuitant, it is a period of loss, danger * * * fall of wages * * * bankruptcy. * * * It means the ruin of all dealers whose debts are twice their business capital, though one-third less than their actual property." In March of 1876, however, Sherman had got ready, as usual, to swallow his words and subvert his record, and he *opposed* the New York Chamber of Commerce—as desired, of course, by English bullionists and American-Tory bankers. As Senator Sherman and Senator Bogy spoke on the same day, Senator Stewart, though a very careful man, fell into the error, in his speech of September 5th, 1893, of attributing Bogy's remarks on demonetization to Sherman. The present writer, who happened to come upon the error, called Mr. Stewart's attention to it, on the 22d of December, and it was corrected by him, in the Senate, the same day.

Five months after Mr. Bogy's speech, John Sherman delivered an address—not indeed in the Senate, but before the inquiring and doubting faces of his Ohio constituents, whom he needed for future use. It was at Marietta, on the 12th of August, 1876, and his words were published *verbatim*—six columns of them—in the organ of his party, the Cincinnati *"Commercial Gazette."* John Sherman said:

"I have given the subject" [the silver question] "the most careful consideration, and WAS THE FIRST TO PROPOSE THE RE-COINING OF THE OLD SILVER DOLLAR. * * * I was a member of the Conference Committee of the two Houses on the Silver-Bill. Both Houses were in favor of issuing the old dollar—the dollar in legal existence since 1792, containing 412 8-10 grains, and *only demonetized in 1873, when it was worth two per cent more than gold*. It was then, and for twenty years had been, only issued for export, and was not in circulation. Still, it was a legal standard of value, as well as gold, always had been, and it was *the right of any debtor to pay in silver dollars as well as gold dollars.* It was his legal option. The relative value of the two metals had often varied before, and still *the right of the debtor remained to pay in either dollar, and therefore in the cheaper dollar.* The mere disuse of the coinage of the silver dollar could not, and ought not, to affect pre-existing contracts. And now, when our domestic contracts have been based upon depreciated paper money made a legal tender for all debts public and private, except customs and duties, and interest on the public debt, it would seem not only legal but *right*, in the broadest sense of the term, that we should avail ourselves of the remarkable and rapid fall in silver bullion *to recoin the old silver coins, including the old silver dollar—the oldest of our coins*—and with them pay our depreciated notes, and thus *restore the old coin standard.*"

Printing John Sherman's Marietta speech, the Cincinnati *Gazette* naturally described him as "a silver-dollar revivalist." According to himself, he was the *first* silver-dollar revivalist—*"the first to propose the re-coining of the old silver-dollar."* At that time John Sherman was not standing up "defending a law" which had been "denounced and vilified"—the act demonetizing silver. He was not "boldly avowing" that he "did read the law" and "knew its contents." He was deprecating that law, as taking away the rights of debtors and interfering with "pre-existing contracts." He was declaring that it "would seem not only legal, but *right*, in the broadest sense," to abrogate that law by re-coining "the old silver coins, including the old silver dollar—the oldest of our coins"—and thus to "restore the old coin standard." In short, *John Sherman was pleading "the baby act,"* and was claiming the honor of being the very *first* to perform that feat. Disavowal of abetting such legislation—a disavowal long made by many of Mr. Sherman's fellow Senators—he now describes as "deception and falsehood, largely the result of cowardice." But, was John Sherman himself a deceiver, a liar and a coward, when, in 1876, he did *precisely the same thing?*

In his speech of August, 1893, Mr. Sherman tells us that the law which in August, 1876, he considered unjust, and unfit to exist any longer, is now "*the great act of* 1873," but "is stained by the imputation of our own countrymen."* Was Mr. Sherman no longer one of "our own countrymen" when *he* stained "the great act of 1873"? Or had he become a virtual subject of England—the American attorney of her great Bank and her Jew bondholders, with their Tory partners in America? Feeding on such clients in 1876, was John Sherman talking merely for "buncombe" —merely to be able the better to serve his patrons in the future? He tells us *now* of England: †

"There is among the nations of the world one great creditor nation, which holds bonds and securities * * * to the amount of thousands of millions of dollars. * * * It is a nation of intelligent people who command the commerce of the world. * * * We ought not to be ashamed of them, or to hate them or dislike them; because we are their children, and possess very many of the qualities of the parent stock."

In this last citation from Mr. Sherman there is not apparent a single falsehood. And, really, Americans are too sensible to "hate" the English as such. Still, in 1876, when Great Britain had influenced the legislation of the United States in a way that "suits England, but does not suit us," it is plain that some of her children, called Americans, possessed "many qualities of the parent stock."

Having informed us eighteen years ago, that what is to-day "the great act of 1873" was an imposition upon the people, the correction of which he had been the first to propose, Mr. John Sherman, in August of 1893, indignantly assures all "falsifiers and cowards" that the same act, "from beginning to end," was "honorable to Congress, free from corruption, open and ingenuous, frank and full."

"What is the history of that bill? [he exclaimed]. It was a bill framed in the Treasury Department. It did not come from Congress in the ordinary way, but was framed in the Treasury Department by a distinguished body of experts. * * * They prepared this bill at the request of the Secretary of the Treasury."

But this statement by John Sherman, like the most of his statements, leads us into great difficulties. How could "a distinguished body" of American "experts," marshaled by a Secretary of the Treasury, frame a bill by which "*the United States was influenced by Great Britain*" and which John Sherman should be "*the first*" to *repudiate?* What kind of "experts" must they have been? And what kind of Secretary of the Treasury must have had them in hand? Were they a lot of rascals, trying to impair contracts, cheat debtors, and help another country against their own? If not, were they a pack of fools? If neither rascals nor fools, why were they "framing a bill" which Senator John Sherman and "both Houses" sought to counteract, and which Senator Bogy pronounced to be a piece of legislation procured by the influence of Great Britain?

The way out of this tangle is easier than one might think. The Secretary of the Treasury in 1870 was Mr. George S. Boutwell of Massachusetts,

* Record, page 920.   † Record, Aug. 31st, pages 916 and 917.

who, in 1876, was a member of our Monetary Commission, and who is described by a fellow member as follows: *

"In Mr. George S. Boutwell we had, for a Secretary of the Treasury a petty shop-keeper, with a shop-keeper's methods—an honest, well-intentioned, dull, heavy, inexperienced, self-sufficient, narrow-minded and thoroughly incapable person, who knew neither the law nor the mechanism of the Treasury, and who consequently became the dupe of every intriguant of his day."

Mr. Boutwell's grasp of the principles of money may be judged, with no waste of time, from the fact that he is a "Cernuschi bimetallist," meaning a man who sincerely believes that America must do business with a currency which settles English balances.† If there were a single peg on which to hang such utter nonsense, the United States would have had no dollar to fight the Revolution, and would be to-day a political dependency of England, with an established church according to Mr. Gladstone's prayer-book. "International Bimetallism" is one of the two infallible tests of economic idiocy—the other being "the intrinsic value of gold." ‡
Following the assertions of John Sherman, we find that "Mr. Secretary Boutwell * * * claims to be the author" of the Mint bill, "and properly so, because he was at the head of the Department." § Still, Mr. Boutwell was only the *Pickwickian* author; for on the 8th of April, 1890, Mr. John Jay Knox, in a letter to Hon. A. J. Warner,|| said, in so many words:

"*I* was the author of the act of 1870, which subsequently became the law of 1878, or at least of that section which discontinued the coinage of silver dollars."

In 1870, Mr. John Jay Knox was Deputy Comptroller of the Currency, but more especially a zealous servant of the National Banks. He was soon after "promoted" to the presidency of the National Bank of the Republic, in New York City; and, according to Senator Stewart, "such promotions of Treasury officials who have been faithful to the banking interests have been too frequent to escape observation."

*Hon. Alexander Del Mar, in a letter written at the Primrose Club, London, Aug. 9th, 1893, and published in the Peoria (Ill.) Journal, Aug. 23d.

†"Inasmuch as balances there [in England] must be settled in gold, it would seem wise for other commercial nations to make that metal the sole standard of value, or by a general agreement, to which England should be a party, secure the bi-metallic standard."—Boutwell's Minority Report, U. S. Monetary Commission of 1876.

‡History has furnished only one instance of a state of unmentality more profound than this. On the 5th of June, 1890, Mr. J. H. Walker, of Massachusetts, told the House of Representatives that "money has no place whatever in economics. * * * You might [said he] destroy all the gold and silver in this country to-night, and waking up to-morrow morning you would not be hurt one iota; our business would go on just the same. * * I do not mean if gold and silver were demonetized and greenbacks put in their place. * * I am talking about the destruction of money out of the world."—To what has Massachusetts fallen! Such stuff as this is not even the product of dementia. Here is catalepsy.

§Sherman, Aug. 30th, '93: Cong. Record, Aug. 31st, page 920.

|Published, with Mr. Warner's celebrated reply, in "Silver in the Fifty-first Congress," issued by the National Executive Silver Committee, 1890.

Now the *whole record* of Senator John Sherman, for thirty years, shows conclusively that, of all servants of the National Banks, with the money-power in general, *he* has been by far the ablest and the most indefatigable. His biography will consist chiefly of bank-acts, the overwhelming appendix being the law demonetizing silver.* So, when Secretary Boutwell—Pickwickian claimant of the "Mint Bill"—tells us that it was "prepared under the supervision of John Jay Knox," we can easily see under what "supervision" John Jay Knox was "prepared." There is no use of mincing matters with the so-called "honorable" John Sherman. His unsupported word is not to be taken on any subject; but when, spurning "the baby act" he "stands boldly avowing" that he "did read" the Mint-act, and "knew its contents," the evidence is such that no reasoning creature can doubt his veracity. Mr. Boutwell's "Mint Bill," prepared "under the supervision of John Jay Knox," was simply, and on its face, a Sherman supplement—elaborate, intricate, ingenious and misleading—to the Sherman bill of 1868, which attempted to demonetize silver *then*, but was silently wiped out by E. D. Morgan. The following extracts from that bill show what it was:†

"With a view to promote a uniform currency among the nations, the weight of the gold coin of $5 * * * shall agree with a French coin of 25 francs; * * * and the other sizes or denominations shall be in due proportion of weight.

"In order to conform the silver coinage to this rate, and to the French valuation, the weight of the half dollar shall be 179 grains * * * and the lesser coins be in due proportion. *But the coinage of silver pieces of one dollar, five cents, and three cents, shall be discontinued.*

"Gold coins to be issued under this act *shall be a legal tender in all payments to any amount;* and the silver coins *shall be a legal tender not exceeding* $10 *in any one payment.*

"The devices of the coins shall consist of such emblems and inscriptions as are proper to the Republic * * * but plainly distinct from those now in use: each coin shall express its proper date and value; and the value of the gold coins shall be stated both in dollars and francs.

"There shall be no charge for coinage, seigniorage, or internal revenue [on gold and silver coins nine-tenths fine, received by weight at the mint]. On all other deposits of gold for coinage the charge shall be one half of one per cent."

Presenting the bill to the Senate (June 9th, 1868), Mr. Sherman urged it as embodying the plan of the Paris Conference of 1867, of which he said:

"It proposes:
1. *A single standard exclusively of gold.*
2. Coins of equal weight and diameter.
3. Of equal quality of fineness. * * *

*Wendell Phillips said it could be reduced to this: "Entered the Senate poor; soon made himself enormously rich."
†Senate Committee Report, No. 117, 40th Congress, 2d Session, pp. 4, 5, 6.

4. The weight of the present 5-franc gold piece to be the unit.
5. The coins of each nation to bear the names and emblems prepared by each, but to be legal tenders, public and private, in all."

It is seen from these citations that the Sherman bill of 1868 conformed a little more technically to England than his bill of 1870, in making silver a legal tender for ten dollars instead of five—the last amount being somewhat worse than the first, for *us*. This bill, not being hidden in the paraphernalia of a "Mint Act," had nothing to do with salaries, penmanship and tinkering, but consisted of ten short paragraphs, instead of the sixty-eight cumbrous sections of the latter bill, which made it about as long as the book of Deuteronomy. But, apart from its masks, shop-truck and kite-tails, the long bill of 1870 was substantially contained in the short one of 1868, even as to minor matters, like emblems, seigniorage, and the discontinuance of small silver coins, all of which subsequently came up for discussion.* Thus Secretary Boutwell, Man-Friday Knox, with all the rest of them, were little more than *names* in connection with the "Mint-Act." They were all held in the hat of John Sherman.

This extraordinary person assures us, at present, that the "Mint Act" was a "scientific bill," sent out in advance to scientific men, and to "everybody who desired to read it," or "could be prevailed upon" to render judgment "in respect to coinage." Hon. E. D. Morgan, not being a "scientific" man, appears to have received no copy of the document, and the same may be said of all the leading Senators and Representatives of States practically interested in the precious metals. Dr. Linderman, Director of the Mint, was favored with a copy: whereupon he recommended to Mr. Sherman's Finance Committee exactly what Mr. Sherman had recommended in a bill two years before—that "the silver dollar," being "of no practical use," its "issue should be discontinued."† Mr. John Jay Knox was not neglected in the distribution of the bill, being under the childish impression that he was the "author" of it. "In the report accompanying the introduction of the bill, April 25th, 1870," Mr. Knox, (then Comptroller of the Currency), informed Mr. Sherman that, in the "Mint Bill," the "present gold-dollar piece is made the dollar unit * * * and the silver-dollar piece is discontinued"—exactly the thing that was done by Mr. Sherman's bill of 1868, so far as silver was concerned.

Beyond Dr. Linderman and Professor Knox, few of Mr. Sherman's "scientific" gentlemen need delay us. They showed at once that he described them without his accustomed mendacity when he said:

"These were men who would rather pore over a table of logarithms or study a problem in geometry * * * than to do anything to tarnish their name and their fame."

*More of this further on. Both bills are given in full by Senator Stewart, in his speech of Sept. 5th, 1893, and are thus easily accessible.
†Record, Aug. 31st, 1893, page 931.

No doubt of it. No one has ever questioned the *character* of those excellent "scientists." They were masters of fluxions, dies and burnishers. They understood *coinage*. Few of them knew anything about MONEY. There was literally but one suggestion from their whole number, having any profound weight for the business world, unless to *injure* it. The officers of the San Francisco Branch Mint asked:

"Would not the proposed change in the weight of the silver dollar disturb the relative value of all our coinage, affect our commercial conventions, and possibly impair the validity of contracts running through a long period?"

The financial brains of the country, so far as they were honest, appear to have "gone West" some time ago.

But, to sum up the preliminary situation in connection with the "Mint Act,' the statesmen, the politicians, and the people of the United States, so far as they ever heard of it, considered it a thing pertaining to the Mint alone, and of *no other consequence*. For this reason, it was never discussed by the press, and it never came to public notice. As for members of Congress—our national law-makers—they had no occasion to give a thought to it in advance, as their business is to think of bills when matured, put into form, and presented to them. They, of course, saw none of the "scientific" reports which went to Mr. Sherman's Committee, and which have been dug up for a new generation; and few men ever read anything emanating from Mr. George S. Boutwell, at any time in his life, without doing their own intelligence the honor of instantly forgetting it. No suggestion, certainly, of his, even if observed, would receive the slightest attention preceding the time of action upon it. General Garfield told the whole story when he said:

"I never read the bill. I took it upon the faith of a prominent Democrat and a prominent Republican, and I do not know that I voted at all. * * * Nobody opposed that bill that I know of. It was put through, as dozens of bills are * * * *on the faith of the report of the Chairman of the Committee.*"[*]

In 1870 our country had no gold and silver in circulation, but had been doing business, since 1861, with paper, and there was no prospect of a return, for years, to metallic money. A "Mint Bill," at such a time, was naturally about as interesting, and seemed about as important, as the inventory of a junk-shop. Finally, here, let us consider this picture of the epoch:[†]

"It appears to be a fact, however humiliating to admit it, that in this country pretty nearly all knowledge of the literature on money had been lost. If there was a

---

[*] Speech at Springfield, Ohio, autumn of 1877. Quoted in Senate proceedings, February 13th, 1878.
[†] From "Silver in the Fifty-First Congress," issued by the National Executive Committee, 1890; General A. J. Warner, Chairman.

man in public life in the United States at that time who had any considerable acquaintance with the literature that arose out of the discussions of the problems of suspension and resumption in England, and subsequent measures leading to the Bank Act of 1844, he made no exhibition of it. Other questions had absorbed the attention of our people, and then came the war. * * * But if ignorance on the question of money prevailed in this country, shrewd observers of the situation were not wanting in other countries. Men trained in the school of Ricardo well understood that, with the vast debts created by the American and the Franco-Prussian wars, if the money-standard of the world could be changed from gold and silver to gold alone, the effect would be to enormously enhance the holdings of creditors and creditor nations; and at this time our national debt was largely held in Europe. Here was the motive, and here the opportunity. *A world was open to plunder.* But * * * change in the money-standard, at such a time and for such a purpose, was simply *an act of spoliation,* no more justifiable in the abstract than *theft or piracy.*"

The "Mint Bill," then—Mr. Boutwell being its putative father, Mr. John Jay Knox being its supervisory father, and Mr. Sherman being the real father of that illegitimate monstrosity—was submitted to the Finance Committee of the Senate, April 25th, 1870, was introduced in the Senate, April 28th, and was thence referred back to the Committee. On the 19th of December, it was brought up again, with amendments, and printed. On the 9th of January, 1871, the bill came formally before the Senate for discussion, in the Committee of the Whole. Mr. Sherman, in his speech of August, 1893—the grandest effort of his life, perhaps, in subversion of the truth—asserts, with great emphasis, that, in a section of the bill enumerating subsidiary silver coins—the half-dollar, quarter, and dime made legal tender for *one dollar*—no mention of the dollar itself, the old constitutional standard, was found. Again we are not obliged to take Mr. Sherman's word: the fact is a matter of record. But this fact was *just the trouble.* Nobody supposed that the standard dollar *would* be included in such a section; and certain papers, specially referring to the point, were not before the Senate, but behind the Chairman of its Committee on Finance. Hence the trick—since stigmatized as such in both Houses of Congress by their best-known members—was not discovered. As Senator Stewart has said,

"The silver dollar was omitted from the list of coins, which omission was not observed, and *the attention of the Senate was not called to it.*"

In the first Senatorial discussion of the "Mint Bill," after two or three trivial matters in relation to salaries were disposed of, one amendment from Mr. Sherman's Committee instantly aroused hot debate. It was this:

"For coinage, whether the gold and silver deposited be coined or cast into bars or ingots, in addition to the charge for refining or parting the metals three-tenths of one per cent."*

* Congressional Globe, proceedings January 9th, 1871, page 368.

Of this suggested amendment, Senator Stewart says:

"[It] was regarded as a direct attack upon the mining industry of the United States, and also upon domestic coinage. It was argued that such a provision of law would discourage the minting of gold and silver in the United States, and encourage its exportation, because the mints of the leading nations of Europe made no charge for coinage after the metal had been refined and parted."

The debate on this proposition went through two days, and occupied fourteen pages of the Globe. On the first day the Senate agreed to it, and on the second day defeated it. The bill itself was then brought up, and was passed by 36 to 14, John Sherman voting *against it*. As the bill had demonetized silver—though without the knowledge of the Senate—and as no silver could be "deposited" in the Mint to "be coined" for its owners, Mr. Sherman has been charged with presenting the amendment *for the deliberate purpose of deceiving his fellow Senators*—diverting their attention from the chief end of the measure, and fixing it on a comparatively unimportant though considerable interest. The wording of the amendment, certainly, is very suspicious; and it served the supposed intent to perfection. But it is not at all sure that Mr. Sherman's purpose was not a double one. In his demonetizing bill of 1868, he put a clause providing that on all "deposits of gold for coinage, [except on pieces of money for re-coinage], the charge shall be *one-half* of 1 per cent."* In his demonetizing bill of 1870, he changed the fee for coinage to *three-tenths* of 1 per cent. Pickwickian author Boutwell, and supervisory author Knox, had not put in any charge at all, as the bill left their hands. Had they forgotten to follow directions? Or had author Knox been let into the secret of a coming subterfuge? Mr. John Sherman, anyhow, insisted, by amendment, on the substance of his former scheme of '68. As "the mints of the leading nations of Europe made no charge for coinage," and as any such charge would "encourage exportation" of the precious metals—repressing the volume of domestic currency just so far—might not a faithful attorney of foreign powers, and of contractive home-bankers, have considered it his duty to procure even a minor advantage for them? It requires careful attention to follow the crooked promenades of the so-called "honorable" John Sherman.

The "Mint Bill," having passed the Senate without the discovery of its being chiefly a thing of false-pretences, went to the House, and to the Committee on Coinage, Weights and Measures, of which William D. Kelley was Chairman. Mr. Kelley reported it, February 25th, 1871, with amendments, and it was recommitted. During the extra session of the Forty-Second Congress, (March 9th, 1871), Mr. Kelley re-introduced the bill, to go to the same Committee, "when appointed." On the 9th of January,

---

* "A Bill in Relation to the Coinage of Gold and Silver," Section 7: Senate proceedings January 6th, 1868.

1872, Mr. Kelley, as Chairman of the newly appointed Committee, reported the bill to the House with no changes later than the preceding February. Practically, therefore, the bill was unnoticed for more than a year after it left the Senate. It had become an "old thing," with the prestige of originating in the Treasury and being approved by the Senate. In this presentation of the "Mint Bill," Mr. Kelley informed the House that the purpose of the measure was to codify and simplify the Mint laws, *the most important change* being to establish a Director of the Mint with headquarters in the Treasury Department. "It is of the highest importance, there-fore," he said, "that the *one single cardinal change that the bill proposes* should be made."

From these remarks, it is evident that Mr. Kelley had not seen the real point of the "Mint Bill," though he declared that "it had received as careful attention" from the Coinage Committee *of the previous year*, as he had "ever known a committee to bestow on any measure."

"The bill, [he added], *has not received the same elaborate consideration from the Committee * * * of this House*, but the attention of each member was brought to it, * * * each member procured a copy of the bill, and there has been a thorough examination * * * again."

Yet Mr. Kelley always maintained, to the day of his death, that he was "ignorant of the fact" that the Mint Bill "would demonetize the silver dollar." That he *was* ignorant of it when making his speech of January 9th, 1872, is proved by a remark to Mr. Potter on that occasion:

"There are one or two things in this bill, I will say to the gentleman from New York, with his permission, which I personally would like to modify: that is to say, I would like to follow the example of England, and make a wide difference between our silver and gold coinage."

The only possible inference from this remark is that the Mint Bill had *not* done what Mr. Kelley favored. Yet this bill, at that time, had *gone further than England herself* in the very direction he specified. No one has ever suspected Mr. Kelley of intentional wrong in this connection. Almost no one, perhaps, without minute inspection of the dry heap of papers which accompanied the bill from the Treasury to Mr. Sherman, would have seen more, at that time, than Mr. Kelley saw; and when "each member" of his Committee "procured a copy of the bill," the now celebrated writings of "author" Knox received no attention that any mortal has heard of.

The good Mr. Kelley's further obscurity of mind was evinced in the following bit of debate:

Mr. Potter. I desire * * * to ask the gentleman who has this bill in charge whether * * * it will make any change in the value of the coin issued * * * from the value of the coin which now exists?

Mr. Kelley. It does not.

Mr. POTTER. Does it make any change in the standard of weight or of fineness of the coin?
Mr. KELLEY. It does not.
Mr. POTTER. Does it provide any new kind of coin; coin of any new denomination other than that which is now coined?
Mr. KELLEY. It does not.

In all his answers to Mr. Potter, Mr. Kelley was more or less in error. He was not even aware that the old American dollar had been dropped, and "the five-franc dollar" put in its place, though no silver dollar at all had been included in the original Treasury scheme, and Mr. Kelley's own Committee had "amended" the dollar into the bill, adding it to the half-dollars, quarters and dimes, which had alone been specified. On the 9th of March, 1878, Mr. Kelley said:

"I do not think there were three members in the House who knew [that the act demonetized the standard silver dollar]. *I doubt whether Mr. Hooper, who, in my absence from the Committee on Coinage and attendance on the Committee of Ways and Means, managed the bill, knew it.* I say this in justice to him."

Ah, HERE WE HAVE IT! Mr. Kelley had relegated the Mint Bill to SAMUEL HOOPER—BANKER—and had merely talked on it, in a perfunctory way, as he was advised. Why not? Mr. Kelley had known Mr. Hooper for many years. Mr. Samuel Hooper, indeed, had been one of that immortal Committee of Ways and Means of which Thaddeus Stevens had been Chairman in 1861. Why should not Mr. Kelley feel perfectly safe in trusting Mr. Samuel Hooper with the details of a non-political, technical "Mint Bill"?

On the 9th of January, 1872, in addition to what we have been over,

"Some discussion was had with regard to the salaries of officers, but the main contention was with regard to nickel coinage, and how the nickel should be obtained. The House adjourned that day without action on the bill.* On the 10th, * * * the House resumed consideration of the bill. The debate was confined to the question of salaries.† No allusion whatever was made to the omission of the silver dollar. The bill was finally re-committed to the Committee on Coinage, Weights and Measures."

According to "author" Knox,‡

"It was again reported, February 9th, 1872, from the Coinage Committee, by the Hon. Samuel Hooper, printed and recommitted, and on February 13th, 1872, reported back by Mr. Hooper with amendments, printed, and made the special order for March 12th, 1872, until disposed of."

* For convenience, this correct summary is adopted from Senator Stewart.
† On this occasion, Hon. Martin I. Townsend of New York, a very practical and quickwitted member of the House, exclaimed: "I move to strike out the enacting clause in this bill, so that we may proceed to *something of which the country is more in need than the discussion of mints and coinage.*" Mr. Townsend's motion actually received 77 votes in its favor, against only 100 noes.
‡ His general report on the history of the Act: printed in the Congressional Record of Aug. 31, 1893, page 923.

At this juncture, according to Mr. McNeeley, of Illinois, the Committee had *not been together*, and *had not authorized the report*.

The bill came up again on the 9th of April. Mr. Hooper made a long speech, explaining and favoring the bill. The " Record," at least, shows such a speech, though various members of the House, then present, have stoutly maintained that Mr. Hooper's remarks were never *spoken*—only *printed*. Mr. Stoughton made a quasi-minority speech—another prepared effort which no one seems to have *heard*—in which he said:

"It [the Mint Act] is a measure which it is hardly worth while for us to adopt at this time. This bill provides for the making of changes in the legal-tender coin of the country, and for substituting, as legal-tender, coin of only one metal instead, as heretofore, of two. *I think, myself, this would be a wise provision*, and that legal-tender coins, except subsidiary coins, should be of gold alone; but *why should we legislate* on this *now*, when we are not using either of those metals as a circulating medium?"

Mr. Hooper and Mr. Stoughton both stated that a reduction had been made in the weight of the silver dollar, and Mr. Stoughton said of the silver coins "they are made a legal tender for all sums not exceeding $5 in any one payment." But, as the silver dollar was at that time worth three and a-half per cent more than the *gold* dollar, his listeners, if he had any, appear to have thought that the "Mint Bill" simply equalized the two different dollars. Even Mr. Kelley, holding about the same view as Mr. Stoughton, said in debate:

"It is impossible to retain the double standard. * * * But, sir, I again call the attention of the House to the fact that the gentlemen who oppose this bill insist on maintaining a silver dollar worth 3½ cents more than the gold dollar, and worth 7 cents more than two half-dollars, and that, so long as those provisions remain, you cannot keep silver coin in the country."

William D. Kelley was a true friend of the American people. He was sometimes taunted with being a "greenbacker"—a "worshipper of the rag-baby." In connection with the "Mint Bill," he doubtless supposed it brought gold and silver to a parity, and that paper-money could do all else that might be needed. The demonetization of silver may yet lead the people to take a short cut to some of Mr. Kelley's most radical views, with small concern for *any metal whatever*.

The debate pursuant to the speeches of Mr. Hooper and Mr. Stoughton became, at last, very warm, not to say hot, and threatened to subject the "Mint Bill" to dissection from beginning to end. The Hon. Clarkson Potter, of New York—a very shrewd and capable man—said:

"The introduction of the bill, at such a period, excited my suspicion. I was and am at a loss to gather from anything I know or can learn, that there is any necessity for the adoption of this measure now. When the bill comes to be read, section by section, I shall make such suggestions, in the way of amendments as I think are calculated to make it better. * * * This bill provides for the making of changes in the legal-tender coin of the country, and for substituting, as legal-tender, coin of only one metal instead * * * of two. I think, myself, this would be a wise provision; * * * but why should we legislate on that now, when we are not using either of these metals as a circulating medium? The bill provides also for a change in respect of the weight and value of the silver dollar, which I think is a subject which, when we come to require legislation about it at all, will demand * * * very serious consideration, and which, as we are not using such coins for circulation now, seems an unnecessary subject about which to legislate. But, beyond that, the bill provides for an entirely new subsidiary coinage. * * * We shall have another set of minor subsidiary coins, of nickel copper, according to * * * this bill. For what reason? * * * It has occurred to me that, behind this provision of the law, lies the real motive power of this bill; that is, that it will make necessary a great consumption of nickel copper, for several hundred million pieces of this new subsidiary coinage."

We see, here, that while the keen Mr. Clarkson Potter had not yet reached the stupendous job behind Mr. Sherman's "great act of 1873," a *job of some kind* was evident to him, and he was on the way to expose it. The debate was closed by adjournment. But the Mint Bill was now in imminent danger. So its agents PRETENDED TO ABANDON IT. They brought in a NOMINAL SUBSTITUTE, and assured the House that it OBVIATED ALL OBJECTIONS; though, as Senator Stewart says, "*no change was made with regard to a single matter objected to in the debate.*"

After setting the controversy to cool for *seven weeks*, the pretended substitute was brought up by Mr. Hooper, on the 27th of May, 1872, *in the absence of Mr. Potter.* In presenting it Mr. Hooper said:

"I do so for the purpose of *offering an amendment in the nature of a substitute*—one which has been very carefully prepared, and which I have submitted to the different gentlemen in this House who have taken a special interest in the bill. I find it meets with universal approbation in the form in which I offer it."

As not one change had been made on one point entering the controversy of April 9th—this being proved by the very face of the bill—what must be said of Mr. Hooper's manner of employing speech? As the "Mint Bill" had inveigled him for some time into close contact with John Sherman, had Mr. Hooper, once clearly an honest man, caught Mr. Sherman's most chronic ailment? Had his tongue been stricken with moral leprosy?

He moved that the rules of the House "be suspended," and "THE SUBSTITUTE be put on its passage."

Hon. James Brooks, of New York, objected.

"I ask the gentleman from Massachusetts, [said he], to postpone his motion until *his colleague on the committee,* my colleague from New York [Mr. Potter] is in his seat. *It is my impression that he does not concur in this substitute.*"

Mr. Hooper declined; and, being urged, declined again.

Mr. Holman said:

"I suppose it is intended to have the bill read before it is put upon its passage."

"The substitute will be read," [replied the Speaker of the House].

"I hope not," [exclaimed Mr. Hooper]. "It is a long bill, and those who are interested in it are perfectly familiar with its provisions."

"I want the House to understand [said Mr. Kerr] that it is attempted to put through this bill without being read."

Mr. Brooks intimated that, not knowing what was "going on," he should vote "no."

Mr. Holman interposed:

"Before the question is taken upon suspending the rules and passing the bill, I hope the gentleman from Massachusetts will explain the leading changes made by this bill in the existing law, especially in reference to the coinage. It would seem that all the small coinage in the country is intended to be recoined."

"This bill [replied Mr. Hooper] makes no changes in the existing law in that regard. It does not require the recoinage of the small coins."

Before the debate ended, Mr. McNeeley rather noticeably atoned for his complaint of a previous occasion, that the Committee had not authorized the bill, by saying now:

"As a member of the Committee on Coinage, Weights and Measures, having carefully examined every section and line of this bill, and generally well understanding the subject before us, I am satisfied the bill ought to pass."

Mr. McNeeley's *style* in this remark, sounds very much as though he had been loaded beforehand for his shot. We do not know. But Mr. Hooper finally succeeded in suspending the rules, and passing the "Mint Bill."

No wonder Mr. Holman said a little later:*

"I have before me the record of the proceedings of this House on the passage of that measure, which no man can read without being convinced that the measure and the method of its passage through this House was A "COLOSSAL SWINDLE." I assert that the measure never had the sanction of this House, and it does not possess the moral force of law. * * * *I myself asked the question of Mr. Hooper, who stood near where I am now standing, whether it changed the law in regard to coinage. And the answer of Mr. Hooper certainly left the impression on the whole House that the subject of the coinage was not affected by that bill.*"

No wonder, again, that Mr. Bright, of Tennessee, indignantly used this very plain language in connection with Mr. Hooper and his "substitute."

"IT PASSED BY FRAUD IN THE HOUSE, never having been printed in advance, being a substitute for the printed bill; never having been read at the Clerk's desk, the reading having been dispensed with by an impression that the bill made no material alteration in the coinage laws; it was passed without discussion, debate being cut off by operation of the previous question. It was passed, to my certain information, under such circumstances that the fraud escaped the attention of some of the most watchful as well as the ablest statesmen in Congress at the time. * * * *Aye, sir, it was a fraud that smells to Heaven. It was a fraud that will stink in the nose of posterity, and for which some persons must give account in the day of retribution.*"

* Speeches in the House of Representatives, July 13th and August 5th, 1876.

Aye, verily: and the day of retribution is at hand.

Mr. Hooper's "FRAUDULENT SUBSTITUTE" for a CRIMINAL "MINT BILL" went to the Senate from the House, the last time, on the 28th of May, 1872; thence into the hands of Mr. Sherman's Committee of Finance; thence back to the Senate, on the 16th of December, with certain amendments, which were printed on January 7th, 1873. These, when presented to the Senate on the 17th, as the record shows,* were patiently considered.

Mr. Sherman said:

"I send to the clerk some amendments of *a formal character* from the Committee on Finance, *adopted since the amendments first reported were printed.* I will ask that they be acted upon, with the others, in their order."

Three verbal amendments were made, applying to sections 5, 8, and 9 of the bill, consecutively. Then a long debate took place in regard to striking out a part of section 14, providing for the reception, by the Treasury, of abraded gold coins. This appears to have been considered an interest special to California, the debate being almost wholly between Mr. Sherman and the two Senators from that State. Finally, one of them, Mr. Casserly, said he should contend with Mr. Sherman no longer, "because" it was "*evident that very few Senators*" *were* "*paying attention to this subject.*" The part of section 14 was stricken out, the rest of it retaining its number and place.

The next section (number 15), *applying to the same subject of abrasion*, looks now as if it had been put into the bill, separately, *on purpose to be dropped.* An amendment to strike it out was successful, after some formal opposition.

The complete omission of section 15 transferred that number to the next section, and put number 17 under 16. The original number 16, now moved back to 15,—and more especially the amendment to it—*was the one which demonetized the American silver dollar, with its full power of legal tender.* The amendment was this:

"The silver coins of the United States shall be a trade-dollar, a half-dollar or fifty-cent piece, a quarter-dollar or twenty-five cent piece, a dime or ten-cent piece; and the weight of the trade-dollar shall be *four hundred and twenty grains* troy; the weight of the half-dollar shall be twelve grams and one-half of a gram; the quarter-dollar and the dime shall be respectively one-half and one-fifth of the weight of said half-dollar; and said coins shall be a legal-tender at their nominal value for any amount not exceeding five dollars in any one payment."

The section and the amendment were alike, except that the amendment substituted a "trade-dollar" for a "five-franc dollar," or one of 384 grains, *neither being the dollar of the United States.*

* Occupying 19 columns of the Globe, and reprinted in full in Senator Stewart's speech of Sept. 5th, 1893.

Here was a very dangerous piece of a "Mint Bill" to be *read aloud*, or even to be *whispered*, however confiding, and momentarily inattentive, might be a Senate whose members supposed they could trust their Chairman of Finance. SO WHAT WAS DONE? The amendment to Section 16, with the section itself, WAS NOT READ AT ALL; but, under that number, the original number 17 was intoned to the Senate, and the sections HAVING BEEN MOVED UP, *nobody noticed the difference.* Only the terrible and infallible notes of the Senate stenographer, giving all the proceedings, word for word, finally uncovered the chicanery and the infamy of that day. The one man who was never known to miss a syllable of the Senate's proceedings, recorded here—A GAP.

On the 5th of June, 1890, the so-called "honorable" John Sherman—in presence of the Senate, with the documents put under his nose by Senator Stewart—was whipped into the absolute necessity of *acknowledging the omission.* But, even then, the conspirator from Ohio attempted to outface the "Record" by saying:

"Because the Reporter does not happen in the hurry of business to catch every amendment in the precise order in which it was presented, the Senator would therefore convict some one of grave wrong."

But the reporter *did* "catch every amendment *in the precise order in which it was presented.*" He caught everything that was said. He merely failed to "catch" a few hundred words, more or less, that WERE NEVER UTTERED.

On such occasions as the one just described, Mr. Sherman and his friends have for some time deemed it best that he should have assistance, Senator Aldrich and Senator Hoar having been the most conspicuous deploy in this service. But in pity, even for a Sherman, something better than this should be done for him. If he seeks counsel to shield him from the monster-crime of the modern world, he should employ a less transparent pettifogger than the manufacturer of Rhode Island, and a more dexterous manufacturer of sophistries than the antique innocent of the Massachusetts bar.

When Mr. Sherman offered to the Senate, for the last reading, his bill "to codify the Mint Laws," he said:

"I rise for the purpose of moving that the Senate proceed to the consideration of the Mint Bill. I will state that this bill *will not probably consume more time than the time consumed in reading it.*"

Mr. Sherman spoke modestly. The bill consumed *less* time than the time that would have been consumed in reading the *whole* of it.

Eight months later, President Grant, whose signature was attached to the "Mint Law," wrote, as part of a letter,

"The panic has brought greenbacks about to a par with silver. I wonder that silver is not already coming into the market to supply the deficiency in the circulating medium. When it does come, and I predict that it will soon, we will have made a rapid stride towards specie payments. Currency will never go below silver after that."

When, in January of 1875, Grant signed the Resumption Act, he advised, in his special message to Congress, the establishment of *more mints to coin silver dollars.* He said :

"With the present facilities for coinage, it would take a period probably beyond that fixed by law for final specie resumption, to coin the silver necessary to transact the business of the country."

We have it on authority of Hon. Edwards Pierrepont, Grant's Attorney General, and subsequently Minister to England, that, after the secret was out, Grant said, in talking the matter over, that he had been "*deceived.*'

But General Grant was not the only man able and distinguished enough to become President of the United States, who knew nothing of the actual contents of the specious "Mint Act," when it was made a law by his aid. General Garfield, as we have seen, said that he "never read the bill." He took it *on the faith of the Chairman of the Committee."* Exactly. James A. Garfield being witness against John Sherman of Ohio and Samuel Hooper of Massachusetts—for the application fits these two men equally —the "Mint Bill" was passed ON FAITH, and THE FAITH WAS BETRAYED.

James G. Blaine was Speaker of the House—a man not apt to be asleep in his chair. Yet he was obliged to say afterwards, when he had become a Senator,

"I did not know anything that was in the bill";

and he added the very significant remark, largely explanatory of the whole imposture:

"Little was *known* or *cared* on the subject."

The *reason* that "little was known or cared on the subject" was clear. Doctor Sherman's "scientific" "Mint Bill," coming from *savant* Boutwell, through Professor Knox, was always represented to Congress as a measure for the sole convenience of great specialists in the Mint and Treasury. Besides, it was a *holy* bill, which Doctor Sherman always treated as if he were superintending a Sunday-school, and which hallowed the trade-dollar with the pious motto : "In God we trust." Why should a layman, and a very practical servant of the people, like Mr. Blaine, pay attention to such a cerulean piece of legislation ? So, in later years, Mr. Blaine necessarily became one of John Sherman's "cowards and falsifiers," whom he has accused of pleading "the baby-act."

At that same moment, Mr. D. W. Voorhees was another—though, in the amicable year of 1893, Doctor Sherman forgave Mr. Voorhees, for the sweet sake of consummating the crime of 1873. But, on the 15th of February, 1878, it was Senator Voorhees who elicited from Senator Blaine his confession, and who said, when asked if *he* knew what the bill was doing:

"I very frankly say that I did not."

We are now aware—if only we could accept a statement from the mouth of a John Sherman—that the Senatorial conversation between Mr. Blaine and Mr. Voorhees was all "deception and falsehood, largely the result of cowardice."

But let us tabulate, as it were, Mr. John Sherman's

"DECEIVERS, FALSIFIERS, AND COWARDS."

The column, partly erected, will stand in this form:

GENERAL U. S. GRANT—President of the United States.
GENERAL JAMES A. GARFIELD—President of the United States.
JAMES G. BLAINE—U. S. Senator.
ROSCOE CONKLING—U. S. Senator.
ALLAN G. THURMAN—U. S. Senator.
DANIEL W. VOORHEES—U. S. Senator.
JAMES B. BECK—U. S. Senator.
WILLIAM B. ALLISON—U. S. Senator.
WILLIAM M. STEWART—U. S. Senator.
TIMOTHY O. HOWE—U. S. Senator.
FRANK HEREFORD—U. S. Senator.
LEWIS V. BOGY—U. S. Senator.
JOHN T. MORGAN—U. S. Senator.
WILLIAM D. KELLEY—Representative in Congress.
WILLIAM S. HOLMAN—Representative in Congress.
JOHN M. BRIGHT—Representative in Congress.
SAMUEL B. BURCHARD—Representative in Congress and Director of the Mint.
JOSEPH G. CANNON—Representative in Congress.
RICHARD P. BLAND—Representative in Congress.

Here are nearly twenty names pretty well known to the American people; but until recently we have never known them to be the names of "deceivers, cowards, and falsifiers," in the habit of pleading "the baby-act." Let us see how they did it. Let us think over their words, as they have left them for our attention:

"I did not know that the act of 1873 demonetised silver. I was *deceived* in the matter."—*U. S. Grant.*

"Perhaps I ought to be ashamed to say so, but it is the truth to say that, I at that time being chairman of the Committee on Appropriations, and having my hands over-full during all that time with work, I never read the bill. I took it upon the faith of a prominent Democrat and a prominent Republican, and I do not know that I voted at all. There was no call of the yeas and nays, and nobody opposed that bill that I know of. It was put through as dozens of bills are, as my friend and I know, in Congress, on the faith of the report of the chairman of the committee; therefore I tell you, because it is the truth, that I have no knowledge about it."—*James A. Garfield, as reported in the Congressional Record, volume 7, part 1, Forty-fifth Congress, second session, page 989.*

" I want to ask my friend from Maine, whom I am glad to designate in that way, whether I may call him as one more witness to the fact that it was not generally known whether silver was demonetized. Did he know, as the Speaker of the House, presiding at that time, that the silver dollar was demonetized in the bill to which he alludes?"—*D. W. Voorhees, Senate, Feb. 15th, 1878.*

" I did not know anything that was in the bill at all. As I have said before, little was known or cared on the subject. And now I should like to exchange questions with the Senator from Indiana, who was then on the floor and whose business it was, far more than mine, to know, because by the designation of the House I was to put the question; the Senator from Indiana, then on the floor of the House, with his power as a debater, was to unfold them to the House. Did he know?"—*Jas. G. Blaine.*

" I frankly say that I did not."—*Mr. Voorhees.*

" Will the Senator allow me to ask him or some other Senator a question. Is it true that there is now by law no American dollar?"—*Roscoe Conkling, in the Senate, March 30th, 1876.*

" I cannot say what took place in the House, but know that when the bill was pending in the Senate we thought it was simply a bill to reform the Mint, regulate coinage, and fix up one thing and another; and there is not a single man in the Senate, I think, unless a member of the Committee from which the bill came, who had the slightest idea that it was even a squint toward demonetization."—*Allan G. Thurman, in the Senate, Feb. 15th, 1878.*

" It [the bill demonetizing silver] never was understood by either House of Congress. I say that with full knowledge of the facts. No newspaper reporter—and they are the most vigilant men I ever saw in obtaining information—discovered that it had been done."—*Senator Beck, January 10th, 1878.*

" I know that the bondholders and the monopolists of this country are seeking to destroy all the industries of this people, in their greed to enhance the value of their gold. I know that the act of 1873 did more than all else to accomplish that result, and the demonetization act of the Revised Statutes was an illegal and unconstitutional consummation of the fraud. I want to restore that money to where it was before, and thus aid in preventing the consummation of their designs."—*Senator Beck again.*

" But when the secret history of this bill of 1873 comes to be told, it will disclose the fact that the House of Representatives intended to coin both gold and silver, and intended to place both metals upon the French relation instead of our own, which was the true scientific position with reference to this subject in 1873, but that the bill afterward was doctored. * * * It was changed after the discussion, and the dollar of 420 grains was substituted for it."—*Senator Allison, Feb. 15th, 1878.*

"It was of no consequence whether or not I knew in February, 1874, that silver was demonetized in February, 1873. It was too late to prevent what had been done in the previous year. * * * I did not know that silver was demonetized for more than a year after February, 1874, since which time my bitterest enemies will hardly blame me for not doing all in my power in and out of Congress to remonetize silver. But the statement of the Senator from Ohio that I knew on the 11th day of February, 1874, that silver was demonetized, or that I said so, has no foundation in fact. The quotation from the speech which he held in his hand when he made the statement does not prove it, and the speech itself disproves any such inference."—*W. M. Stewart, Senate Speech, Sept. 5th, 1893.* *

"Mr. President, I do not regard the demonetization of silver as an attempt to wrench from the people more than they agree to pay. That is not the crime of which I accuse the act of 1873. I charge it with guilt compared with which the robbery of two hundred millions is venial."—*Senator Howe, Feb. 5th, 1878.*

"I say that beyond the possibility of a doubt (and there is no disputing it) that bill which demonetized silver, as it passed, never was read, never was discussed, and that the Chairman of the committee who reported it, who offered the substitute, said to Mr. Holman, when inquired of, that it did not affect the coinage in any way whatever."
—*Senator Hereford, Feb. 13th, 1878.*

"Why the act of 1873, which forbids the coinage of the silver dollar, was passed, no one at this day can give a good reason."—*Senator Bogy, of Missouri.*

"Did the people demonetize silver? Never! It cannot even be fairly said that Congress did it. It was done in a corner darkly. It was done at the instigation of the bondholders and other money kings, who now, with upturned eyes, deplore the wickedness we exhibit in asking the question, even, who did the great wrong against the toiling millions of our people?"—*Senator Morgan, Dec. 13th, 1877.*

"I have before me the record of the proceedings of this House on the passage of that measure, a record which no man can read without being convinced that the measure and the method of its passage through this House was a 'colossal swindle.' I assert that the measure never had the sanction of this House, and it does not possess the moral force of law."—*Mr. Holman, in the House, July 13th, 1876.*

The original bill was simply a bill to organize a bureau of mines and coinage. The bill which finally passed the House and which ultimately became a law was certainly not read in the House. * * * It was never considered before the House as it was passed. Up to the time the bill came before this House for final passage the measure had simply been one to establish a bureau of mines; I believe I use the term correctly now. It came from the Committee on Coinage, Weights and Measures. The substitute which finally became a law was never read, and is subject to the charge made against it by the gentleman from Missouri [Mr. Bland], that it was passed by the House without a knowledge of its provisions, especially upon that of coinage. I myself asked the question of Mr. Hooper, who stood near where I am now standing, whether it changed the law in regard to coinage. And the answer of Mr. Hooper certainly left the impression upon the whole House that the subject of the coinage was not affected by the bill."—*Mr. Holman, in the House, Aug. 5th, 1876.*

* The first *honest* man in America, perhaps, who knew of the demonetization of silver, was General A. J. Warner, who learned the fact in April, 1874, *in London*, from the venerable Samuel Lang, afterwards a member of Gladstone's Cabinet.

"This legislation was had in the Forty-second Congress, February 12, 1873, by a bill to regulate the mints of the United States, and practically abolished silver as money by failing to provide for the coinage of the silver dollar. It was not discussed, as shown by the *Record*, and neither members of Congress nor the people understood the scope of the legislation."—*Joseph G. Cannon, in the House, July 13th, 1876.*

"The Coinage Act of 1873, unaccompanied by any written report upon the subject from any committee, and unknown to the members of Congress who, without opposition, allowed it to pass under the belief, if not assurance, that it made no alteration in the value of the current coins, changed the unit of value from silver to gold."—*Mr. Buchard, of Illinois, in the House, July 13th, 1876.*

"All I can say is that the Committee on Coinage, Weights and Measures, who reported the original bill, were faithful and able, and scanned its provisions closely; that as their organ I reported it; that it contained provision for both the standard silver dollar and the trade dollar. Never having heard until a long time after its enactment into law of the substitution in the Senate of the section which dropped the standard dollar, I profess to know nothing of its history; but I am prepared to say that in all the legislation of this country there is no mystery like the demonetization of the standard silver dollar of the United States."—*Judge Kelley, in the House, May 10th, 1879.*

Mr. Bright's indignant remarks in the House of Representatives, in which he said that the "Mint Bill" passed "*by fraud,*" and that it would enter the nostrils of posterity with a direful odor, have been noted, and need not be repeated. One more citation shall close this list of Mr. John Sherman's victims to their various execrable characteristics.

"The silver dollar is peculiarly the laboring man's dollar, as far as he may desire specie. * * * Throughout all the financial panics that have assailed this country, no man has been bold enough to raise his hand to strike it down; no man has ever dared to whisper of a contemplated assault upon it; and when the 12th day of February, 1873, approached, the day of doom to the American dollar, the dollar of our fathers, *how silent was the work of the enemy! Not a sound, not a word, no note of warning to the American people that their favorite coin was about to be destroyed as money; that the greatest financial revolution of modern times was in contemplation and about to be accomplished against their highest and dearest rights!* The taxpayers of the United States were no more notified or consulted on this momentous measure than the slaves on a southern plantation before the war, when their master made up his mind to increase their task or to change them from a corn to a cotton field. Never since the foundation of the government has a law of such vital and tremendous import, or indeed of any importance at all, crawled into our statute books so furtively and noiselessly as this. Its enactment there was as completely unknown to the people, and indeed to four-fifths of Congress itself, *as the presence of a burglar in a house at midnight to its sleeping inmates.* This was rendered possible partly because the clandestine movement was so utterly unexpected and partly from the nature of the bill in which it occurred. The silver dollar of American history was demonetized in an act entitled ''An act revising and amending the laws relative to the mints, assay offices and coinage of the United States.''—*Senator Voorhees, January 15th, 1878.*

If we now recur, for an instant, to Mr. Kelley's remarks, just quoted under date of May 10th, 1879, we shall see that "in all the legislation of this country," he conceived there was "no mystery equal to the demonetization of the standard silver dollar." Some light has since been thrown on that "mystery." On the 9th of April, 1872, Samuel Hooper, *banker*, to whom Mr. Kelley had confidingly entrusted the "Mint Bill"—made the following observation on the floor of the House:

"MR. ERNEST SEYD, OF LONDON, a distinguished writer, who has given great attention to mints and coinage, after examining the first draft of the bill FURNISHED MANY VALUABLE SUGGESTIONS, WHICH HAVE BEEN INCORPORATED IN THIS BILL."

Some further reference to Mr. Ernest Seyd appears below, in the form of an affidavit.

STATE OF COLORADO, } *ss.*
COUNTY OF ARAPAHOE,

Frederick A. Luckenbach, being first duly sworn on oath, deposes and says: I am 62 years of age. I was born in Bucks county, Pennsylvania. I removed to the city of Philadelphia in the year 1846, and continued to reside there until 1866, when I removed to the city of New York. In Philadelphia, I was in the furniture business. In New York, I branched into machinery and inventions, and am the patentee of Luckenbach's pneumatic pulverizer, which machines are now in use generally in the eastern part of the United States and in Europe. I now reside in Denver, having removed from New York two years ago. I am well known in New York. I have been a member of the produce exchange and am well acquainted with many members of that body. I am well known by Mr. Erastus Wyman.

In the year 1865 I visited London, England, for the purpose of placing there, Pennsylvania oil properties, in which I was interested. I took with me letters of introduction to many gentlemen in London—among them one to Mr. Ernest Seyd from Robert M. Foust, ex-Treasurer of Philadelphia. I became well acquainted with Mr. Seyd, and with his brother, Richard Seyd, who, I understand, is yet living. I visited London thereafter every year, and at each visit renewed my acquaintance with Mr. Seyd, and upon each occasion became his guest one or more times—joining his family at dinner or other meals.

In February, 1874, while on one of these visits, and while his guest for dinner, I, among other things, alluded to rumors afloat, of parliamentary corruption, and expressed astonishment that such corruption should exist. In reply to this, he told me he could relate facts about the corruption of the American Congress that would place it far ahead of the English Parliament in that line. So far, the conversation was at the dinner table between us. His brother Richard and others were there also, but this was table talk between Mr. Ernest Seyd and myself. After the dinner ended, he invited me to another room, where he resumed the conversation about legislative corruption. He said: "If you will pledge me your honor as a gentleman not to divulge what I am about to tell while I live, I will convince you that what I said about the corruption of the American Congress is true." I gave him the promise, and he then continued. "I WENT TO AMERICA IN THE WINTER OF 1872-73, AUTHORIZED TO SECURE, IF I COULD, THE PASSAGE OF A BILL DEMONETIZING SILVER. IT WAS TO THE INTEREST OF THOSE I REPRESENTED—THE GOVERNORS OF THE BANK OF ENGLAND—TO HAVE IT DONE. I took with me £100,000 sterling, with instructions if that was not sufficient to accomplish the object to draw for another £100,000 or as much more as was necessary."
He told me, GERMAN BANKERS WERE ALSO INTERESTED IN HAVING IT ACCOMPLISHED.

He said he was the financial adviser of the bank. He said: "I SAW THE COMMITTEES OF THE HOUSE AND SENATE AND PAID THE MONEY AND STAYED IN AMERICA UNTIL I KNEW THE MEASURE WAS SAFE." I asked if he would give me the names of the members to whom he paid the money—but this he declined to do. He said: "*Your people will not now comprehend the far-reaching extent of that measure—but they will in after years.* Whatever you may think of corruption in the English Parliament, I assure you I would not have dared to make such an attempt here, as I did in your country." I expressed my shame to him, for my countrymen in our legislative bodies. The conversation drifted into other subjects, and after that—though I met him many times—the matter was never again referred to.

   (Signed)   FREDERICK A. LUCKENBACH.

Subscribed and sworn to before me at Denver, this ninth day of May, A. D. 1892.

   (Signed)   JAMES A. MILLER,
[SEAL]   Clerk Supreme Court, State of Colorado.

The affidavit of Mr. Frederick A. Luckenbach is not an agreeable thing to incorporate in any American publication. But is it *true?* That is the only point of much account, in the end.

The exact history of the affidavit may assist us in judging.

It appeared, for the first time, in the *Rocky Mountain News*, a very able and influential journal edited and published by Hon. T. H. Patterson, of Denver, Colorado—a lawyer and orator as well as editor, and one of the best-known men of the West. It was inserted with this introduction:

"Mr. Frederick A. Luckenbach is a citizen of Denver, and is well and favorably known by many of Colorado's leading business men. He has been engaged for two years past in introducing his pneumatic pulverizer, and has met with flattering success. It having come to the ears of Mr. M. H. Slater, chairman of the executive committee of the State Silver League, that Mr. Luckenbach possessed the startling information contained in the affidavit, that energetic gentleman immediately waited upon him and induced him to put the whole story in explicit form and give it to the public. This Mr. Luckenbach did, and the result is the affidavit published below."

In other words, Mr. Luckenbach had spoken of this matter in conversation with friends, and it had got out. Dr. Slater, a prominent physician, and the President of the Colorado State Silver League, was naturally interested in it. He saw Mr. Luckenbach, and asked him if the report of his conversation was correct. Assured of its being so, Dr. Slater persuaded Mr. Luckenbach to repeat the story in detail, which he did in the presence of Mr. Patterson. When urged to put it into form and subscribe to it, on the ground of its public importance, Mr. Luckenbach said he would do so, if his friends deemed it advisable; but, being a business man, in no way connected with public affairs, he would rather not. He acceded, however, to Dr. Slater's request, and the affidavit was prepared. Mr. Patterson, Dr. Slater, and Mr. James A. Miller, Clerk of the Supreme Court of Colorado, give entire credence to Mr. Luckenbach's assertions,[*] which have been

---

[*] This information was imparted to the writer, a short time ago, by Mr. Patterson himself, as also by Hon. G. C. Merrick, Dr. Slater's successor as President of the Colorado State Silver League.

submitted, also, to General Warner, and others of high position, who, on careful inquiry, find no reason whatever to doubt them. Mr. Luckenbach, in short, is a citizen of Denver, a native American, a man of character, means, and large business connection, both in his own country and in Europe. His long and friendly acquaintance with Ernest Seyd is *undisputed*.

Mr. Luckenbach's deposition reached the Eastern States, after a fashion, through printed slips bearing this statement:

"The above is clipped from the *Rocky Mountain News* of May 12, 1892. It is circulated in this form for the reason *that the Associated Press refused to handle it east of Denver*.   M. H. SLATER,
President Colorado State Silver League."

What better evidence is required, than this simple item, to prove that the American Press, so far as concerns its great combination of "metropolitan journals," is nothing but a pack of muzzled dogs, that bark or hush as they are whipped and fed by the bank-and-bullion trust? A most immediate, a most pressing need of the people in this country, is to protect themselves and their children from the poison of what William Lloyd Garrison used to call, in his day, "the Satanic press." It is more "Satanic" now than it was then, and on a much larger scale. The present task on which it is employed, is so to confuse the public mind, on the all-important question of MONEY, that "the land of the free and the home of the brave" shall be reduced to a workhouse of paupers and a field of serfs. The means chiefly employed to this end are two—MISREPRESENTATION and SUPPRESSION. But fortunately, a considerable part of the "country press" declines degradation, at any price, and has not been subsidized and prostituted. The extraordinary light thrown by Mr. Luckenbach upon the demonetization of silver spread through the country, and finally glared in Congress. IT HAD TO BE NOTICED. Then "the leader of the gold-trust," as the so-called "honorable" John Sherman has been called by Senator Stewart, gave out, through the attorneyship of his henchman, Mr. Hoar, a long letter from Ernest Seyd himself to Samuel Hooper.* The letter bears date of February 17th, 1872—seven weeks after which Mr. Hooper made his reference to Ernest Seyd in the House of Representatives. In presenting the letter to the Senate, Mr. Hoar said:

"It begins by saying that Mr. Hooper has forwarded to Mr. Alfred Latham, who I think was *a governor of the Bank of England*, a copy of the coinage bill proposed for the United States, and requested to have it sent to Mr. Seyd for his criticism. The writer of the letter discusses, as a master of the subject, various practical questions, among them the proper size of gold-pieces. * * * But Mr. Seyd then goes on to say that the *fifteenth section of the bill* is the part which after all is of the *greatest importance*. He says it is a matter of *gigantic importance;* that it is THE GREAT QUESTION

* Published in the Congressional Record of August 23d, 1893.

OF THE CENTURY. He avows himself earnestly in favor of the free coinage of silver at the ratio of 14 to 1, a little less than the rate then existing in the United States. * * * He implores Mr. Hooper to reconsider the subject, and says the great fault of Mr. Hooper's bill is that *it abolishes the coinage of the silver dollar with the full legal-tender quality;* and he says that America, being a producer of both metals, is the nation upon which the world must depend to resist *the enormous danger which menaces mankind by the threat of adopting the single gold standard.*"

Ernest Seyd's letter to Mr. Hooper is a very long one. "It covers," as Mr. Hoar tells us, "twenty-eight or thirty foolscap pages," and it occupies four pages of the finest print of the "Congressional Record." It contains, that is, about twelve thousand words. It is all that Mr. Hoar claims for it, and a good deal more. It shows that Dr. Sherman's "scientific men" of 1870, under Professor Knox, in the Treasury and the Mint, were, comparatively speaking, infants in a nursery. But it evinces deep and true feeling, as well as incomparable ability. Mr. Hooper had written:

"As to the theory of the double valuation, I do not understand it."

Mr. Seyd explained it to him fully, so that a school-boy could comprehend it, and impressed upon him the supreme fact of all, that the single standard of metallic money was *impossible,* as there was not "*gold enough in the world*" to make it honest, humane and practicable.

"Men like yourself, [said he], on framing a coinage bill, undertake a gigantic responsibility, which strongly affects, not only a whole nation's welfare and happiness, but also that of the world at large. Pray do not despise this language. The deep study of all the principles and interests connected with the organization of social life warrants it."

Mr. Hooper was earnestly reminded that the "Mint Bill," by making silver a legal-tender for only five dollars, was even "more severe" than the English system, which gives a debt-paying power of ten dollars to that money. In justice to the humble poor of the world, and specially in justice to the masses of the United States, Mr. Seyd recommended *the free coinage of silver, with the full legal-tender function;* but he begged Mr. Hooper, if that should not be attainable, to give to the metal the legal-tender of at least fifty or a hundred dollars, that honest industry might pay modest debts with it.

No one can read that letter from Ernest Seyd without seeing that he was naturally a true man with a good heart. According to Samuel Hooper, we remember, Mr. Seyd's communication "furnished many valuable suggestions" which had "been incorporated" in the "Mint Bill." That Samuel Hooper could read the letter, could make such a statement with reference to it, and could then smuggle through the House of Representatives a bill *containing every diabolism against which Ernest Seyd had protested,* renders any suspicion of bribery between them a matter of complete insignificance. If that letter had been called to the attention of Congress in 1872, or if *any honest use* had been made of it, there would have been as little possibility of demonetizing silver as of stealing from the heavens their silvery clouds. Samuel Hooper is lost forever, AS A TRAITOR TO HIS COUNTRY.*

Of Ernest Seyd, it must be added, here, that, as long as he lived, he continued to advocate the cause of bimetallism. Let us say it with more emphasis.

"Ernest Seyd was one of the ablest champions of silver produced in Europe during this century. In fact he laid down his life on the altar of silver * * * by rising from a sick bed, when he was unfit to be up, and going to attend the Paris Monetary Conference of 1881, where he died in harness." †

Then how could Ernest Seyd have become the conveyor of a bribe from the Bank of England and German bondholders to the Congress of the United States? THERE STANDS HIS CONFESSION, under oath of a friend, with permission to give it to the world in due time. The publication has been made, and those who know the friend accept it as genuine and authorized. What is the solution of the two facts, Seyd's letter to Hooper, and Seyd's confession to Luckenbach? It is simple enough. A scholarly and guileless gentleman, Mr. McCleary of Minnesota, put the substance of this question, not long ago, in the House of Representatives, to the wise and experienced "Uncle Joseph Sibley," of Pennsylvania. Mr. McCleary wanted to know if the man who used the language of Ernest Seyd could have done the thing attributed to him.

"Yes, sir, [replied 'Uncle Joseph '], I have seen men sell out within the last two months. * * * I have known men to change their minds within twenty minutes. Wise men, it is said, change their minds often; fools, never."‡

Ernest Seyd was no disburser of bribes, in ordinary circumstances, and was a *sincere bimetallist*. But he was also "*the financial adviser of the Bank of England*"; and the Bank of England had *a larger interest in the demonetization of American silver than any other single institution in the world*.§ England, as a nation, or rather Britain as an empire, had at stake thousands of millions of dollars in depriving American silver of its monetary value, and reducing it to a commodity. To German stock and bond holders, it was worth hundreds of millions, if it could be made effectual and lasting. Ernest Seyd was himself *a banker*. Samuel Hooper's letter

* It is pitiable that Samuel Hooper must be finally summed up for history in this way—the same Samuel Hooper who, in 1861 and '2, stood as upright for the people as Thaddeus Stevens himself. What a monument is Samuel Hooper to the corrupting influence of his National-Bank Association, and to the putrifying companionship of John Sherman!

† Extract from a speech in the House of Representatives by a Mr. M. N. Johnson, of North Dakota, Aug. 24th, 1893. Published in the *Record* of Aug. 31st.

‡ Speech in the House, August 18th, 1893.

§ Our next chapter will explain why.

to him was sent through *Alfred Latham,* one of the shrewdest, hardest, most English *mono-*metallists in Europe. Ernest Seyd, as a *man,* doubtless wrote, on his first normal impulse, his superb reply to our recreant son of Massachusetts; but Ernest Seyd, as *" adviser of the Bank of England,"* was forced to postpone his theories, when that huge octopus came to see its fat prey in the United States. He was in a difficult position. For *the time,* he was serving his country, his friends and his blood, as against a country that England, at heart, still regards as a rebel to her throne and policy.* With *his* prophetic vision, he could see that while the right must ultimately prevail, a rich young nation could be forced to divide its prosperity with Europe and India. Ernest Seyd is not to be altogether blamed. At most, he is only to be blamed as we blame the unfortunate Major André, whom Washington hanged with heart-felt sorrow. André was a true *Englishman*; and so, by position, was Seyd.†
AMERICANS were the VILLAINS in the crime of 1873.

WHO WERE THEY? We may never know, in full, till the Day of Judgment. They are largely hidden beneath the political *débris* of twenty years. The so-called "honorable" John Sherman claims that the Luckenbach affidavit is manifestly false—proves itself to be false—because the "Mint Bill" had "passed both Houses" of Congress "before the time this man says Mr. Seyd came here."

" Mr. Hooper probably invited him to come here, [says Sherman], but it must have been after this letter [from Seyd] was written. * * * And now, according to this anarchist [Luckenbach], he [Seyd] came here and bribed Congress in the winter of 1872-'73, with $500,000 to do what both Houses had done before! This is the way the thing stands now, because the bill had passed both Houses before Seyd could have come here."‡

Does John Sherman dream that he can impose such rubbish as this upon the anuals of his epoch? What confidence he must have in the weakness of the American mind! The fraudulent "Mint Bill" *had* passed both Houses—by means of deceit and falsehood—before Ernest Seyd came here to complete the crime. But it had *not passed the Senate for the last time,* and it was *more or less suspect in the Coinage Committee of the House,* as shown by the proceedings both of April 9th and of May 27th, 1872. The language of Mr. Luckenbach's affidavit in no way implicates the members of Congress in general. His oath, for Ernest Seyd, is this:

" I saw the *Committees* of the House and Senate, and paid the money, and stayed in America until I knew the measure was safe."

---

* Any one who has lived in England, and talked freely with all classes of people—as the writer has done—has quickly discovered this truth.

† It was his sensitiveness as an English subject, we must remember, which prompted his talk with Mr. Luckenbach. But he probably *desired* the world to know the facts, *ultimately.* He was in no sense a *little* man.

‡ Sherman's speech of August 30th, 1893.—Cong. Record, August 31st.

It was not until **January 17th, 1873,** that the "Mint Bill" stole through the Senate, by aid of John Sherman, and by the most audacious piece of chicanery ever known to the annals of legislation. Then, according to the report of "author" John Jay Knox:

"The bill was sent to the House, and on January 21st, 1873, on motion of Mr. Hooper, it was again printed with amendments, and subsequently committees of conference were appointed consisting of Messrs. Hooper, Stoughton and McNeeley of the House, and Senators Sherman, Scott and Bayard of the Senate. The reports of the committees of conference were agreed to, and the bill became a law on February 12th, 1873, substantially as originally prepared at the Treasury."

Thus we see from Mr. Sherman's own "supervisory author" of the "Mint Bill," that the House of Representatives, *as a body*, gave their attention to it, last, when they were lied to and cheated on the 27th of May, 1872, and that the Senate, *as a body*, gave *their* attention to it last, when they were treated still more disreputably on the 17th of January, 1873. *All beyond lay with the Committees*, and was a mere formality, with no inspection. Here was just the time and the opportunity of the Bank of England and its German allies. Previously, no "governor" of that bank, in his senses, could have imagined that a "Mint Bill," with no American dollar in it, could have got on so far without detection and death. For the Bank of England, with its adjuncts, a hundred millions of dollars would have been a small fee for the services desired at just that crisis. No wonder the great value-sucking squid of Europe was willing to pay half a million, or "as much more as was necessary."

It is useless now, to dwell on *names*. Mr. Sherman and Mr. Hooper we know sufficiently. Mr. Bayard, having alway been more or less connected, as clerk and politician, with August Belmont, the Rothschilds' American agent, the Senator from Delaware would have hardly needed any honorarium for prompt service to either a slave or a money oligarchy. An aristocrat from the cradle, his heart has never been in any interest of the people. Senator Scott was a railway magnate, busy enough, probably, with his own particular affairs, to leave a scientific "Mint Bill" entirely to the great gold-specialist, Doctor Sherman, with any particulars of seigniorage that might be attached to it. Mr. Stoughton had persistently declared that such a bill should not be passed at such a time, and Mr. McNeeley had at last become very officious in its favor for his size and weight. But these may have been as "honorable men" as Brutus and Cassius when they murdered Cæsar. It looks as if the most of the filings and clippings connected with the Mint Act were attracted to one or two central magnets. The precise facts are of little moment.

But why should the Bank-Senator from Ohio be so extremely sensitive on a really small matter connected with a career like *his?* Why should he affirm his virtue so strongly as to upset all veracity in doing it? Or the 30th of August, 1893, John Sherman said, in the United States Senate:

"Mr. President, there has been an invention of a story in connection with Ernest Seyd. I suppose Senators have often heard of the story. Some fellow * * * whose name I do not remember, made an affidavit that he knew Ernest Seyd; that he had often met him at his own table; had often dined with him; and, at one time, when they were in conversation, he said that the Parliament of Great Britain was corrupt. Mr. Seyd then said 'they were nothing like the Congress of the United States; that it is the most corrupt body that ever existed.' * * * Seyd said he would tell him a secret, if he would pledge himself never to reveal it while he (Seyd) lived. He promised to wait until Seyd died. Thereupon Seyd said to him that he had raised a fund of £100,000 in the winter—now mark the time—of 1872-'73 to bribe Congress to demonetize silver; and, with a wink, he conveyed to this man, whoever he was, that he had done it. * * * Mr. President, such a story as that, told under these circumstances, would be hooted at by any lawyer, or any honest man. Unfortunately for him, the man, as all rogues are apt to do, gave himself away; for, in the end of this letter, *he declares himself an anarchist, opposed to all governments and all property;* and yet he made an affidavit of this kind, which has no legal force or effect. It is falsified in every single line and word."

Let us waste no time on John Sherman as a low-comedian in the Senate, imitating, "*with a wink*," something that had never occurred. But the affidavit of Mr. Frederick A. Luckenbach is printed in these pages, *exactly as written and signed*. "Unfortunately" for Mr. Sherman, "the man" does *not* "give himself away" as "rogues are apt to do"; does *not* "declare himself an *anarchist*"; does *not* say that he is "*opposed to all governments and all property*"; but he states just the reverse of what Mr. Sherman attributes to him, so far as any statement is made at all of his own antecedents. John Sherman's pretended citation of Mr. Luckenbach is a LIE—a very "cheap and nasty" lie—and is moreover the dodge of a rat in a corner, fighting for a dirty life. But *John Sherman* DOES "GIVE HIMSELF AWAY." Referring to the Luckenbach *affidavit*, the demoralized Senator calls it "*a letter*": it is "the *end of this letter*" from which he gets his twaddle about anarchy. Now the end of the letter to the New York "Graphic," from "HIPPOLYTE GRENIER," gives the author's reason for writing it thus:

"I am a Red Republican in my heart. I believe in the solidarity of the people—in fraternity—in the splendid future in which Europe will be one great republic."

When John Sherman *verbally counterfeited* the Luckenbach affidavit, he could see that by use of the Grenier letter, and by claiming a mistake, he could crawl out of his falsehood, through another, when caught. It was a "tentative" falsehood, like what he calls his "tentative legislation" on the money-question. Both are equally worthy of him.

THIS LUCKENBACH AFFIDAVIT came up again in the Senate on the 28th of September, 1893. But the special subject of consideration was a misquotation of Mr. Samuel Hooper's allusion to Ernest Seyd on the 9th of April, 1872. The misquotation is this:

"Ernest Seyd, of London, a distinguished writer and bullionist, is *now here*, and has given great attention to the subject of mints and coinage; and, after examining the first draft of the bill, made various sensible suggestions which the committee accepted and embodied in the bill."

The words, "*now here*," are not to be found in the Congressional Record giving Mr Hooper's speech of April 9th, 1872, and the whole citation is so loose-jointed in diction that it appears to have been first published by some one from memory. But it has been "going the rounds of the papers" for many years, many persons having used it with perfect good-faith, though careful writers, with access to large libraries, have long avoided the error. But, on the 28th of September, 1893, Mr. Sherman's "ancient," Mr. Hoar, brought it up and exploded it with due pomp and ceremony.* It has no bearing whatever upon Mr. Seyd's being in America *during the winter of 1872 and '3*—hence no bearing on Mr. Frederick A. Luckenbach's deposition. On the same occasion, however, Mr. Hoar incorporated in the Senate's proceedings a letter from Mr. Seyd's son—also named Ernest Seyd—in which the young man says:

"Statements have been circulated for some time past in the press of the United States that the late Mr. Ernest Seyd went to Washington in 1872 * * * in order to bribe members of Congress to vote for the demonetization of silver. I trust you will allow me to assure you the story is an entire fabrication, Mr. Seyd never having been in the States since 1856."

In making this averment, it is probable that the younger Mr. Seyd purposed two good things—to defend his father's memory and to state the truth. But that the elder Mr. Seyd—who was accustomed to attend monetary conferences and the like all over the world, and who finally died while away from home—did not always communicate his entire business to children, was very soon rapped into the wise noddle of Senator Hoar, on the occasion of his great moral splurge, when he denounced misquotation of Samuel Hooper as the unspeakable turpitude of "a squash-bug." Various Senators having defended the purity of Congress, and the "rich" and "lovable" old gentleman, Samuel Hooper, Senator Allison took part in the debate.

"I want to say now and here, [said the Senator from Iowa], that in my belief Mr. Samuel Hooper, of Massachusetts, was as incapable of being in any way influenced or controlled by money as any man who has sat in this Chamber or the other for twenty years. * * * The bill which became the act of 1873 was a sort of pet of his for a

* I myself pointed out the error, several weeks before this event, to a gentleman prominently connected with the Congressional Library One likes to see mis-statements go out of the way.—G C.

year or two. *I would have said that Mr. Ernest Seyd was here in 1873, but for the contradiction made by his son, who states that he was not here at that period of time. I was under the impression that he was here during the Spring of either 1872 or 1873.*"

At this point Mr. Sherman interjected:

"The Senator got that idea from the extract which has been read."

" *I am not quite sure of that* [replied Mr. Allison]. *I was here in the winter of 1872, I think, or in 1873. I am not certain, but I was under the impression, and I may have so stated, that* I MET MR. ERNEST SEYD HERE. Until the statement by his son I believed that he had been here at that time."

"He has not been here since 1856," [said Mr. Cullom]

"He was not here *when the bill passed*," [replied Mr. Allison]. What I desire to say is, that Mr. Ernest Seyd was here in any respect connected with the passage of the bill I do not believe; and, if he was here, he was here accidentally. His attention may have been called to the bill by Mr. Hooper *at that time*."

In other words, Ernest Seyd *was* in America in 1872 or 1873, and Mr. Allison *met* him, according to the Senator's *memory*, and according to what he "*may have stated*"; but the most prudent of Senators is too parliamentary, too polite, to contradict, in direct terms, on the floor of the Senate, the letter of the younger Mr. Seyd. When, in 1878, Mr. Allison declared that the "Mint Bill" had been "*doctored*," he added, "if I may use that term, and I use it in no offensive sense—it *was changed after discussion*." Mr. Allison's memory is quite correct in regard to his meeting Mr. Seyd, and is quite correct also in regard to his having "so stated." Even David A. Wells, in a plea for the gold-trust as patent as anything ever written, says:

"There was a man by the name of Seyd, and he was in this country in 1872."[*]

There are other men than Mr. Allison and Mr. Wells who remember Mr. Seyd; and, if his presence in America in 1873 had not been well known, those who now pretend to question it would never have waited twenty years, to stand on a misquotation of the "Congressional Record" which *they themselves had always accepted as true*.[†] Mr. Seyd moved

---

[*] Article entitled "The Downfall of Certain Financial Fallacies," published in "The Forum" of October, 1893.

[†] Until very lately no one has ever expressed a doubt on this point. On the 1st of September, 1877, the New York *Tribune*, through a Washington correspondent, had this to say: "General Thomas Ewing in his speech at Columbus, on Tuesday evening, [August 21st], opening the Ohio campaign for the Democrats, says: 'After the European money-kings had stricken down silver in Germany, they sent Mr. Ernest Seyd to the United States, and had our Congress demonetize it also.' At about the same time that General Ewing made this assertion, General A. J. Warner, in the first edition of his "Appreciation of Money," (Henry Carey Baird & Co., Publishers, 1877), said: "The *Banker's Magazine* for August, 1873, contains this important item: "In 1872, silver being demonetized in France, Germany, England and Holland, a capital of one hundred thousand pounds ($500,000) was raised, and Ernest Seyd, of London, was sent to this country with this fund as the agent of the foreign bond-holders and capitalists, to effect the same object, which was successful." The *New*

prominently in Washington for a time, with a generous display of wealth, but quietly. His name was naturally kept out of the local papers, though he ran some risk of putting it on file. For instance, the Washington "National Republican" of January 18th, 1873, contained this item:*

"The Coinage and Mint Bill, passed by the House at the last session, was up in the Senate yesterday, and, after the adoption of several amendments, passed. *An eminent foreign banker gives it as his opinion that the bill as it came from the House was the most effective step that had been yet taken toward the resumption of specie payments.*"

Now "the House bill" here referred to, simply *prevented* silver from being of any use in "the resumption of specie payments," by robbing it of its legal-tender value, and confining its debt-paying power to *five dollars*—a course against which "the eminent foreign banker," Ernest Seyd, had vigorously protested when he first knew of it from Samuel Hooper. In regard to "*resumption*," the House bill and the Senate bill were *exactly alike*. But, when Mr. Seyd visited Washington in 1873, "the eminent foreign banker" was recommending the "Coinage and Mint Bill" for just what he knew it would NOT DO. In short, the one "eminent foreign banker" who had been consulted in the matter, (by way of the Bank of England), was not now dealing in the *truth*, but was putting in his controlled and crooked work of afterthought and attorneyship.

During the Senatorial discussion just noted, Mr. Voorhees said:

"I was going to say pleasantly to the Senator from Ohio that I trust he will have better luck than some of us have had in killing falsehoods. They will live long after you think you have destroyed them. They will spring up and look at you next year, and a year on."

Mr. Voorhees need give himself no trouble about Mr. Sherman's luck "in killing falsehoods," *other than his own*, which are practically innumerable. It is the truth alone that John Sherman has to fear, and *that* will be very apt "to spring up" and "look at" him, "next year, and the year on," and while there is a bar of history behind mere "senatorial courtesy" and the mush of relaxed morality.†

York "Banker's Magazine" now contains no such item. On personal inquiry of General Warner, I learn that, within a year or so after the "Mint Act" became a law, he certainly cut the extract from one of the current financial publications of the day—either from some one of the various Banker's Magazines, or from some similar source which *referred* it to "The Bankers' Magazine." Later, the quotation was used by Mrs. S. E. V. Emery in her "Seven Financial Conspiracies," and she has been roundly abused, (even in Congress), for misquotation, but with no real ground, as the facts here evince. I will add that I have in my possession positive written testimony, of *the highest possible character*, that Ernest Seyd was in Washington in 1873, whatever may have been the purpose of his visit. This testimony I do not now publish, for the simple reason that I cannot do so without betraying personal confidence.

* The issue is preserved in the Congressional Library.

† By way of contrast with Mr. Voorhees, we may note that, in a brief letter to the New York *Tribune*, published December 20th, 1877, the venerable Thurlow Weed, on the strength of a communication received from John Jay Knox, announced the wish to apologize for

On the 30th of March, 1876, three years after John Sherman had demonetized silver, Roscoe Conkling asked him one day in the Senate, with astonishment:

"Is it true that there is now by law no American dollar?"

"I will answer the Senator from New York, [said Sherman], that *since* 1853, the use of the silver whole dollar has been discontinued, and none has been issued."

Mr. Conkling persisted, and asked if there was no longer power, by law, to issue the American dollar.

"There is no power, [replied Sherman], and has been none."

Twenty-six days after the Sherman colloquy with Conkling, the same Ohio Senator said:

"The act of 1873 did not in the slightest degree demonetize silver. * * * The right to coin the silver dollar, which is now proposed to be authorised again, has always existed in this country; has never been taken away. * * * The act of 1873 simply leaves the old dollar where the law of 1853 left it. It says nothing about it."*

On August 12th, of the same year, John Sherman said:

"I was the first to propose the recoining of the old silver dollar * * * the dollar in legal existence since 1798, containing 412 8-10 grains, and *only demonetised in* 1873, when it was worth two per cent more than gold."

What is the use of holding converse with John Sherman? What a babe and a suckling were Ananias and Sapphira, compared with their progressed disciple of the Ohio gentiles! If this man had received an official commission as Deceiver-General and Betrayer-in-Chief of the American people, how could he have served them with greater infidelity!

In the act of demonetizing "the American dollar," while pretending to give to it for convenience the value of the five-franc piece—a dollar which he had just dropped altogether by "*doctoring*" the proceedings of the Senate—this monstrosity of sin and impudence said:

"In order to show this—[the equal value of the dollar and the five-franc piece]—wherever our silver coin shall float—*and we are providing that it shall float all over the world*—we propose to stamp upon it, instead of our eagle, which foreigners may not understand and *may not distinguish from a* BUZZARD * * * the intrinsic fineness and weight of the coin."

---

having expressed the opinion that the bill had passed by improper and dishonorable manipulation in Congress. Mr. Weed based his change of view wholly on the specious, technical pretense of Knox that demonetization "originated" in the Treasury. At that time there were no facts to prove that "author" Knox, so far as he "originated" the Mint Bill, was himself "originated" by John Sherman. Thus an old-fashioned, honorable gentleman, like Mr. Weed, was easily imposed upon. Both his mind and heart, however, were so naturally clear, that he still insisted, in a powerful letter published in the *Tribune* of January 10th, 1878, that silver was "*wrongfully* demonetized," and that "the wrong must be righted." "All schemes and laws," he added, "having for their object the repudiation of silver money, will encounter a resistance equally indignant and inflexible."

* *Cong. Record* for April 25th, 1876.

So *foreigners* might not distinguish the American eagle from a buzzard! In this instance a Senator's *lie* about floating all over the world a dollar that he was leaving out of existence, sinks into insignificance in the open filth of his fling at the emblem of his country's freedom. Who but a worse than Benedict Arnold *could* utter such an insult to the American people? A picture of John Sherman is said to be hung up among the portraits of the Bank of England. Hereafter, as "foreigners" look at that picture, they will know the American buzzard. The eagle never roosted there.

Whatever other men may have done, or for any consideration may have left undone, five persons will always stand connected with upsetting the monetary connection of forty centuries between gold and silver, so far as concerns the United States, and of robbing the people of purchasing and debt-paying power to the extent of thousands of millions of dollars. These men are—

George S. Boutwell,
Henry R. Linderman,
John Jay Knox,
Samuel Hooper,
and
John Sherman.

Of Mr. Boutwell, no one may ever impugn the motives. To be like Byron's character who had a "head," but "never knew much what it was about" is not sinful, but only sad. Having given formal notice of his own opinions touching the "Mint Bill," Mr. Boutwell might have honestly thought that somebody beyond the Treasury and the Mint would read them, and that a public official of his dignity was not required to give private information to law-makers who might not agree with him. Granting him a certain combination of narrowness and conceit, there appears to be no need of questioning his integrity.

Of John Jay Knox, history will take small account, whatever he may have done. He called himself the "author" of the Mint Act. So, too, the late General "Tom Thumb," after taking a thimble-full of peppermint and water, used to claim that people might say what they liked, but it was *he* who led the Union forces to their great *defeat* at the battle of Bull Run. Mr. Sherman's "supervisory author," Mr. John Jay Knox, is safe from pursuit. In a hunt for catamounts, fishworms escape.

Mint-Director Linderman knew the contents of the bill relating to his department, and his name will not be fragrant in the annals of his epoch. His writings show that he measurably understood the effects of the demonetization of silver, and sided with conspirators and monopolists against mankind. But did he repent before he died? So we near. Then let us have the same touch of sorrow for him as for one of old, who, having sold his Lord and Master, went out and hanged himself.

In the eyes of various Senators of the United States, Samuel Hooper was "honorable" and "incorruptible"—above reproach. He appears to have had no need of any bribe, though rich men in America, as we see every day, are often the most avaricious and corrupt. Did he receive money from the Bank of England, for adding to its profits on American silver and abstracting the difference from his own countrymen? Perhaps not. Being a BANKER, he *may* have acted his part merely that he might be energetic in attachment to his own special monopoly—a scarlet creature that had long required all sorts of debasement. But why did Samuel Hooper perpetrate a "FRAUD"—a SWINDLE—a "COLOSSAL SWINDLE," as Mr. Holman properly termed it—upon the House of Representatives, in putting through the infamous "Mint Bill"? Why did he present it for the last time, on the 27th of May, 1872, with his mouth full of false pretenses? There is no doubt on that point, and there can be no dodging it, while the "Congressional Record" is extant. Is swindling—the swindling of a House of Representatives and a whole people by a trusted legislator—any better than seduction through a bribe? Let Senators of the United States discriminate in their laudations, or the people will conclude that the higher human faculties are not compatible with public life. The Roman soldier of the Senate, Mr. Stewart, is supremely right, in saying that "*honesty is banished from the world when the crime of* 1873 *is justified.*" *

Looking at the approach to this crime from Paris in 1867, at the scheme to demonetize American silver in 1869, and then at what Mr. Voorhees has called the "stealthy and treacherous" bill of 1870, which was finally "doctored" through the Senate in 1873, who, with eyes, can fail to see that the Lucifer of the whole infernal machinery was our American bankers' political attorney, usually termed "the Senator from Ohio"? As the attorney of foreign bankers as well, did he chiefly centralize the fund of Mr. Ernest Seyd's European syndicate? His case, certainly, has not been helped, of late, by his paroxysms of denial; for these have been possessed with more devils of untruth than were ever needed to pitch swine into the sea. Up to date, Mr. Frederick A. Luckenbach's affidavit stands perfectly good—somewhat strengthened by attack in the United States Senate —and John Sherman's only rejoinder is a shout of "anarchist," as false as all the rest of him. But the mere bribe, again, is of no consequence: the case is so bad that burglary, arson, and murder, might be added to it, with no appreciable increase of wickedness. It long ago led to, and took in, all other sins. But the Mephistopheles of the Senate is supposed to be one of the richest men in the United States, on the "savings" of a salary of five thousand dollars a year.

With a large picture of John Sherman, a little-giant of a paper in Colorado† recently called attention to him in this way:

*Conclusion of speech of June 1st and 2d, 1892. †The Denver "Road."

"Hate is a hard word, and we use it advisedly and with regret; but we hope the fathers and mothers of the rising generation will take their toddling little ones upon their knees, and by the light of the fire in the stove teach them to HATE the face of the man whose picture we herewith publish. He has broken more hearts, caused more suicides, brought about more business wrecks, done more to kill Americanism among Americans, caused more prostitution, starved more children, broken more farmers, wrecked more American homes, and made more money for himself, than any other man that ever sat in the United States Senate."

The Denver paper is right. For men like the one it portrays, we may yet have to supplement our day of Thanksgiving and of Decoration with a solemn day of EXECRATION; and, on that day, as an object-lesson to our children, teach them to curse the enemies of their country.

It is well that William Tecumseh Sherman, greatest but one of all the great generals who marched out to save the Union, lies fast asleep in his country's flag and the glory of his sacred tomb. No less harm in the world than he did good, no less disgrace than for him reverence, stand at the door of JOHN Sherman.

CHAPTER XIII.

EFFECTS OF THE CRIME OF 1873.

THAT THE BANK OF ENGLAND should be anxious to pay half a million dollars, and "as much more" as might be "necessary," to demonetize silver in the United States, is easily understood. Every bank in the world doing business on the British system, and especially the one omnivorous monster of all, has a direct interest in limiting the volume of basic money, and then inflating it with bank-credit. Again, those who are specially represented by the great central English bank are enormous bondholders. We know what these men want, whether Jews or Gentiles: it is to increase the demand for what they own—the gold that must be had to pay to themselves the interest and principal of national debts. Once again, as representing the English Government, the Bank is an agent for the purchase of American silver at the lowest possible figure, as material for whatever silver-coin may be turned out at a profit to the realm. But the Bank of England is connected, directly or indirectly, with all the great credit and bullion dealers throughout the world. So it was not at all necessary that the Bank *alone* should foot the bill of Ernest Seyd. He told his friend Luckenbach that others were interested, calling them "Germans." Certainly. The same Jew-bankers that, since 1816, have been behind the scheme of demonetizing half the metallic money of the world, would never be left out of this last "operation." It is well known that the ROTHSCHILDS are the heaviest dealers of the world in SILVER BULLION. It is they who furnish the material for changes of oriental money-systems, as in

China and Japan. It is they who were back of the drain on American gold and silver from 1851 to 1863—when nearly four hundred and eighty millions went out of the country—and again from 1864 to 1876, when nearly seven hundred and seventy millions followed. A few years ago—in 1888—the report came from China that these Rothschilds had made a secret contract with the Emperor, to substitute silver coin for copper; and, in 1889, the Viceroy of the empire, Li Hung Chang, put up a mint at Canton, to effect the purpose. It was estimated that, if the Chinese were to have even three dollars a head in silver money, the Rothschilds would require the world's entire silver-product for ten years. These thrifty bullionists hope, of course, that they can always get silver in America for a fraction of its true value. If they can find John Shermans enough, their prospects are favorable.*

But the direct returns to Britons and Hebrews, for the demonetization of American silver, are only the smallest consequences of that stupendous crime, with the motives for it abroad. England pays for wheat, corn, cotton—ALL THE GREAT AGRICULTURAL STAPLES THAT ARE PRODUCED IN INDIA—with silver rupees, for which she has been obliged to have the American metal, notwithstanding the common superstition that Europe has had a "surplus of silver." This superstition is simply an importation from London, to supply a demand for deception by New York gold-bugs and their credulous victims. All surplus silver went long ago to Asia. —Professor Jevons's "sink of the precious metals"—and London has been able to bear down American silver only by issuing *paper money*—which she could do to the extent of a few millions of "India Council-bills," put in the place of our product. Free-coinage of the American dollar would have ended this *juggle* at any moment. But our SILVER having been forced down by England to a commodity, cheap for HER GOLD, the English gold-trust has enabled, or rather driven, India, to undersell the United States in the produce-markets of Europe. Are some Americans so limp of mind as to doubt the fact? *Englishmen* are not. In June, 1886, the British and Colonial Chambers of Commerce having convened in London, Sir Robert N. Fowler, the distinguished banker and former Lord-Mayor of the city, told them this:

---

*An excellent summary of this business may be found in the Washington "National View" of July 15th, 1893, from the pen of Jesse Gilmore of San Diego, California, who has given very careful attention to the matter. The "Atlanta Constitution" of January 20th, 1894, had this to say in the same direction:—"According to a recent writer on the subject, China has a per-capita circulation of $1.80, and India a per-capita of $3.44—all in silver. In another ten years, these two countries, at their present rate of progress, will require a per-capita circulation as large as ours, and, as they will never give up silver, it is a reasonable estimate to say that China will require ten billions four hundred millions of dollars, while India will need seven billions eight hundred millions. Now if the world's silver output reaches two hundred millions a year, it would take ninety-one years to produce enough to answer the needs of India and China."

"The effect of the depreciation of silver must finally be *the ruin of the wheat and cotton industries of America, and the development of India as the chief wheat and cotton exporter of the world.*"

At the Second National Silver Convention, at Washington, another Englishman, and one of the best monetary authorities in the world—Mr. Móreton Frewen—said:

"While many intelligent people here are not always alarmed at the imaginary dangers of free coinage, they do not always recognize the immense importance to your farmers of higher rates for silver—they do not recognize that *whenever the price of silver falls, the price of wheat, cotton, and other produce must fall also*. This is a question to which, when in India, I gave very close study, and I should like to make this general statement, which I am convinced the expesience of the past and of the future will amply confirm. Let me put it briefly in this way ; the price of wheat in this country is its price in London or Liverpool, less the cost of carriage from here there, and the London price of wheat is, under ordinary conditions, one ounce of silver per bushel of wheat. Your farmers will always have to sell a bushel of wheat, say in Chicago, for an ounce of silver less freight charges in London ; if then, silver is worth $1.29 per ounce, the London price of American wheat is a dollar and twenty-nine cents, while, if silver is worth ninety cents, then your wheat will only realize ninety cents. This it a statement that will bear close examination, and it is the sum of the importance of the silver question to your nation."

In other words, India—that enormous possession of Britain—has between two and three hundred millions of simple-minded people—more simple-minded, even, than the present generation of Americans who read our "metropolitan press"—and those sad-eyed millions of Asia comprehend no money but the silver rupee. They have always been accustomed to take two-and-a-half rupees, coined from an *ounce of silver*, for *a bushel of wheat*, and can be made accustomed to no other equivalent. When American silver was money—all of it that could be brought to the mint for coinage—its free-coinage money-right made it worth one dollar and twenty-nine cents an ounce, and England had to pay that price for silver. It cost her trade just so much for the material to make the two-and-a-half rupees, to buy the bushel of wheat. But we, having been "influenced by Great Britain," as Senator Bogy said, and having done the demonetizing act that "suits England, but does not suit us," *our silver* could be bought by England so that she could make two-and-a-half rupees for half the old cost. Thus she could get her wheat from India for fifty or sixty cents a bushel, according to the value of silver as a *"commodity,"* and competition obliged our farmers to work down to that level, so far as they could keep from sinking under their mortgages. Such being the case, no wonder that an American farmer has, in some respects, elucidated this whole affair better than any one else who has thus far grappled with it. The farmer is also one of the ablest members of the House of Representatives in Congress—Hon. Joseph C. Sibley, of Pennsylvania. In his justly celebrated speech of August 18th, 1893, Mr. Sibley said:

"My friends, we are told that the Treasury, and the country through the Treasury, has lost vast sums of money in buying 70-cent silver and storing it in our vaults. * * * How much have we lost? Have we lost anything? Every ounce in the Treasury bought below $1.29 an ounce, its coinage value, is so much gain. * * *

But, supposing we had been loser. Supposing, Mr. Speaker, that we had as a government chartered one of the ocean greyhounds sailing from New York, and had loaded every ounce of silver in the country that has been produced since 1873 to the present time, had bought that silver for $1.29 an ounce, and had that ship to sail just off beyond the banks of Newfoundland, and gone into sufficiently deep water where you could not reach soundings, and sunk it to the depths of the ocean, where it would have remained forever beyond the reach of man—what would have been the effect on the producers of the United States?

The highest production of silver in any year has been $78,000,000. We will say it is $75,000,000. But we produce 450,000,000 bushels of wheat a year, which, since the demonetization of silver, has fallen from $1.20 to 54 cents per bushel. The American farmers have lost from 60 to 70 cents a bushel on wheat. The price has gone down because England can come here and take 70 cents' worth of silver and measure it against a bushel of wheat in India, just as well as she could do when it was worth $1.29, before we demonetized it by legislation, and degraded and disgraced it by our wicked follies. Now, then, Mr. Speaker, we have a loss of 50 cents a bushel on wheat—I want to make my statement modest. We have a loss of 50 cents a bushel on 450,000,000 bushels of wheat a year, which makes a loss to the American farmer of $225,000,000.

I am not here talking for the silver-mine owners of Idaho, Colorado, Nevada, Montana and Utah. I do not know them. *They are only a small factor in this question.* I am looking to the producers of wheat and corn, cotton and tobacco, and all the wealth of the nation. We have lost $225,000,000 each year in the value of wheat. Why, if we had bought that 75,000,000 ounces of silver and sunk it in the depths of the sea, so that England could not have got it at 70 cents per ounce, the American wheat-grower would have been a gainer of $225,000,000 annually. We produce 2,000,000,000 bushels of corn, and corn has fallen 26 cents a bushel. Wheat is the great staple, the great leader, and corn is but a follower of wheat among the cereals. Now, then, I will say that we lost 20 cents a bushel on corn, and so our American growers of corn have lost $400,000,000 annually upon their crop of corn, so that if they had bought all this silver and sunk it, the corn-growers would have been $325,000,000 to the good.

We produce 3,213,000,000 pounds of cotton annually, and in 1873 your cotton sold at 23 cents a pound. To-day it is bringing 7 and 8 cents. You have lost 12 cents a pound on every pound of cotton: and if the cotton-producers had bought all the silver and sunk it in the depths of the ocean they would have been each year $210,000,000 ahead on the transaction. In these three leading articles of production in the Union (I will not go through more of them) the loss to the producer each year has been $910,000,000 more than the value of the silver that it would have been necessary to have purchased."

NEARLY A THOUSAND MILLIONS OF DOLLARS A YEAR lost to the United States and gained by Britain, on *three American products, apart from silver, by demonetizing that metal!* * Here we have the most comprehen-

*As this result has nothing to do with opinion, but is one strictly of mathematics, the attorneys of the gold-trust have seldom touched it, though some occasional barrator, (fee unknown), has pretended not to see it. Moses who long ago rejected all there is in the Bible

give motive of all, for the mission of Ernest Seyd to the land of our Tory-Saint of the Whited Sepulchre, John Sherman.

ALL classes of PRODUCERS, however, not excepting the richest, are victims, in greater or less degree, to the crime of 1873. None have complained of it more bitterly than the great manufacturers of Pennsylvania. Their official organ, for instance, "The Manufacturer," contained, in its issue of July 29th, 1893, the following article:

"RESULT OF A BRITISH CONSPIRACY.

"'The assertion made in these columns lately, that the movement for the complete demonetization of silver was the result of *a British conspiracy to obtain from us at unnaturally low prices the cotton, wheat, silver and other commodities produced by us, is fully sustained by the following letter written to an American in New York by Mr. Robert Lacy Everett, a member of the British Parliament:*

'The one great supreme aim of the moneyed classes and the London press is to restrict the supply of money so as to enrich the owners of it at the expense of the raisers of produce and the owners of land and other real property. We hope that the sharp intelligence of your people, in the main a nation of producers and land owners, will see through the cruel game of the moneyed classes and frustrate it. The miseries of the agricultural classes here are indescribable, but they do not clearly see why it is that their prices are forced down to their ruin, so that it is difficult to get them to move. The wits of the American farmers are sharper. I hope our salvation will come from *you.*'

"Whether 'the wits of American farmers are sharper' or not, may be uncertain. It is difficult, upon any hypothesis, to account for the fact that Congress has steadily resisted for years the clamor for abandonment of silver. But either the *wits of American* EDITORS *are not sharp,* or these persons *have deliberately lent themselves to promotion of the British purpose to feed Englishmen and to run English cotton mills at the expense of the American people, and to enhance the value of every debt owed to Britain by Americans.* Gold monometallism and free trade both are devices prepared by Englishmen for injuring other nations for British advantage, and so eager are the plunderers for their prey that they are willing even to sacrifice their own agricultural population and their own agricultural industry that they may filch from their American victims the substance of the latter."

And now for

A FURTHER RESULT OF THE SAME CONSPIRACY.

In the year of our Lord 1893, the schemers of Contraction, from all the banks and Wall-streets known to Satan, filled the world with raving, with wailing and gnashing of teeth, over a certain compromise money-act of the United States, called "the Sherman Law." This law, notwith-

---

can be hired cheap to repudiate arithmetic. It was Macaulay who said that, if the Copernican astronomy had interfered with the money-class, it would have been utterly denied and rejected. In justice, however, to *uninformed honesty,* it is well to bear in mind the recent remark of Sir George Chesney, that "the world is now divided into two money-schools, the bimetallists and the monometallists"—which means into ' those who understand the question, and those who don t."

standing the name of it, had injected a small amount of silver money into a ruinously scant volume of currency, and had thus held off, to some extent, the strangulative effects of the gold-plot, which had been twenty years in culminating. The howl for the "unconditional repeal" of this act, so far as the least scintillation of intelligence stirred behind it, was a howl, pure and simple, from the gold-caves, for a further chance to pillage values. It was a noise at once so wolfish and so brainless—so clearly a cry of brutes for blood—that bankers themselves, of the better class, turned round with disgust, in some instances, and exposed it. In one of the weekly circulars, of Messrs. A. R. Chisolm & Co., Bankers and Brokers of 61 Broadway, New York City, they addressed their correspondents and the public in this way:

"The repealers propose to cure the disease of contraction by more contraction. * * * *More contraction is madness*. It means half a million more idle men in the next sixty days. It means silver down to 40 cents, and wheat down to 50 cents, and cotton at 3 cents. These figures will shut up every bank west of Chicago. THE GOLD-TRUST BANKERS RULE THIS COUNTRY, *not by guns, but by a corner in gold*. Their little game is, making silver buy less and gold more, to cheapen the price of India wheat and cotton, so that this country, on the single gold-basis, must sell these products below the cost of production."

But all this has long been so clear to Americans of intelligence, who have not been deprived of the facts by a pestilential press, that "the breezy West" has even turned the tragedy now and then into comedy, as did Hon. Thomas Fitch of Nevada at the St. Louis Silver Convention of 1889.

"That nation, [said Mr. Fitch], which consumes fifty per cent and produces but seven per cent of the world's supply of silver, beguiled the nation which produces nearly fifty per cent and consumes twenty-five per cent of the world's supply of silver, into a conspiracy to strike thirty-five per cent from the value of silver. That nation which is the greatest importer of wheat in the world, inveigled the nation which is the greatest exporter of wheat in the world, into a financial and commercial dead-fall where thirty-five per cent was taken from the value of wheat. The nation whose looms would be idle, and whose people would be hungry, and whose government would be upheaved upon a storm of riot if without a supply of American cotton, deceived the nation which is the greatest producer of cotton, into striking thirty-five per cent from the value of cotton. Why, gentlemen, *England is the bunco-steerer of the world; and Uncle Sam is the gentleman from the rural districts*."

For a bird's-eye view of the general effects of demonetizing silver, nothing can be better than the following extracts from that vest-pocket cyclopædia of the money question, by General A. J. Warner, modestly entitled "Facts About Silver."*

"LAW OF VALUE OF MONEY.

"The value of gold depends upon the quantity of gold in the world as compared with its use—not its use in the arts alone nor its use as money alone; but all its uses

---

* Published by the American Bimetallic League, Sun Building, Washington, D. C.

combined. If 60 per cent of all the gold in the hands of man is devoted to monetary use and 40 per cent to other uses, then 60 per cent of its value comes from its use as money, and 40 per cent from its other uses—that is, the demands upon the stock of gold would come from these uses, and the effect of each on the value of gold would be in proportion to its intensity. The same law governs the value of silver; and, generally, *the value of money depends upon the quantity as compared with its use, or the demand for it.* THIS IS THE FUNDAMENTAL LAW OF MONEY, *and the most important law in economics.* The conditions which determine need for money, or demand for it, are population and wealth—that is, *number of people to make exchanges and the quantity of things to be exchanged.*

"THE EFFECT OF SILVER DEMONETIZATION.

"The first effect of demonetizing silver was to set up the single gold standard and then to *augment that standard by increasing the value of gold.* The value of gold was increased by increasing its use as money at the same time that its production fell off. In 1873 neither the United States, nor Germany, nor Italy, nor Holland, nor Norway, nor Denmark and Sweden used gold, but after silver was demonetized *all* these countries, containing a population of 150,000,000 of people, adopted the gold standard and went to using gold; and in ten years these seven states took $1,200,000,000 of gold, so that the gold money then in use was divided up among more than twice as many people as used gold in 1873, while the production of gold fell off from a maximum of $155,000,000 in 1853 to about $105,000,000 in 1890. On the other hand the world's population is increasing more rapidly than ever before. The population of the United States doubles in a period of about thirty-four years. There is no prospect of an increase in the supply of gold, while its use in the arts and dentistry increases every year. With the single gold standard, what other result is possible than for gold to go on increasing in value from year to year and prices continue to fall?

"CHANGE IN THE VALUE OF LAND.

"Great as has been the fall in agricultural products, the fall in the price of farm lands has been greater still, notwithstanding the fact that the area of arable land, relatively to population, is rapidly decreasing; and nowhere has the value of land fallen more than in the old settled parts of the country.

"LOSS SUSTAINED BY FARMERS.

"At the price of wheat in 1873 the value to the farmers of the crop of 1893 would have been $455,000,000, instead of $178,000,000, a difference of $277,000,000. This would have gone a long way toward paying off mortgages.

"The corn crop of 1893, at the price of 1873, would have yielded $660,000,000, instead of $412,000,000.

"The cotton crop of 1893, at the price of cotton in 1873, would have been worth to the South $496,000,000, instead of $184,000,000, its actual value in 1893.

"The difference in the value of farm products in 1873 and in 1893 correctly marks the difference between prices with free coinage of silver, as well as gold, and prices as measured by the single standard of gold. The value of farms and farm lands has fallen even more than farm products.

"It is not easy to calculate the loss to farmers and planters in the twenty years from 1873 to 1893 by the fall in value of farms and farm products, as the direct result of THE CHANGE IN THE MONEY STANDARD. Their ability to pay debts and taxes, at any rate, has been reduced in the exact ratio to the fall in prices.

"EARNINGS OF LABOR.

"The earnings of labor, counted in money, have been reduced also. While many things which the laborer uses have fallen with his earnings, taxes, debts, cost of education, and many other things have not been reduced, the net result being a proportional loss to labor; the greatest loss being, perhaps, in loss of employment and consequently in the total earnings of the laboring class.

"THE EXTENT OF THE FALL OF PRICES.

"The extent of the fall in the general range of prices cannot be exactly stated, but tables made at different times by Soetbeer, Saurbeck, Palgrave, the London Economist, and various tables in this country, brought down to 1893, show an average fall of prices of from 38 to 45 per cent, which is equivalent to a rise in the purchasing power of gold of from 50 to 80 per cent.

"*That is, on an average, three to three and a half measures of everything, or three to three and a half days' labor, must be given for the same quantity of gold which two measures or two days' labor would obtain before silver was demonetized.*

"WHAT THE EXCLUSION OF SILVER FROM THE MONEY SUPPLY OF INDIA AND UNITED STATES MEANS.

"For ages, India, with a population of 270,000,000 of people, has derived her money supply from imports of silver which has been converted, without limit, into rupees for the benefit of the holder.

"In the United States, since the passage of the Bland-Allison Act in 1878, from twenty to fifty million dollars of silver a year have been added to our money volume. The total increase in the money volume since 1878, from this source, has been nearly $600,000,000. This is now shut off entirely, and money supply for all Europe, Australia, India and the United States is limited to gold, while at the same time, including Austria-Hungary, which within the same year has decreed the gold standard, more than three hundred and fifty millions of people have been added to those competing for gold ! !

"Is it possible that such a tremendous change can be made in the monetary condition of the world without unsettling everything? Such a disturbance in the money standard in so short a period of time was never known before in the whole history of the world, and we have as yet but seen the beginning of the consequences that must follow this change. The *pricing instrument* has thus at last been completely changed from gold and silver to gold alone, while gold, under present conditions, must rise in value faster than ever, which means that prices must go down faster and go lower than ever. But the number of dollars required to discharge debts and pay taxes will not be less. How long will it take under such conditions for those who own the money and the debts of the world, to own the world? At the same time nearly all the gold is hoarded in a few great banks and treasuries and is controlled by, at most, a few hundred men. * * *

"*While the mints were open to the coinage of silver, the people had a source of supply of money that could not be controlled by combinations of banks. But this is the case no longer.*"

SO MUCH for the physical, the material, the industrial consequences, of the great crime of 1873. But the *moral* consequences of that crime are more shocking and sickening still. It has almost rotted the blood of the world, so far as its leaders are concerned, with the scrofula of dishonesty.

We remember the disclosure of Hippolyte Grenier in the New York *Graphic*, as early as 1876:

"An immense fund was raised to bring about the general adoption of the gold metal basis. The money-writers and political economists of London, Paris, Berlin, Frankfort and Amsterdam, were either argued into the adoption of these views or were purchased outright. Hence the articles in the leading papers of Europe in favor of the gold basis."*

" Of course," added Monsieur Grenier,

"The object of the great capitalists is quite apparent in the crusade against silver. By reducing the currency one-half it would add enormously to their wealth, by cheapening products and giving them a still greater monopoly of the circulating medium."

Having not merely *millions*, but literally THOUSANDS OF MILLIONS at stake, England, Israel, and American-Torydom, combined, have purchased all the literary puddlers of economics in the known world, so far as their brains have been in the market. Some years ago when the "GREENBACK" movement achieved sufficient prominence to be an educative force in the politics of the United States, the American Association of Bankers were accustomed to send out mendacious and malicious matter to such newspapers as they wished to hire for stabbing the truth, and to order the drippings of their poisoned dirks printed as "editorial," and "the bill forwarded." The Chicago *Inter Ocean*, the New York *Sun*, with some other journals which refused to take off the last vestige of common honesty, exposed the bank-assassins, instead of obeying them. But where are nearly all "the leading journalists"? How well they are whipped in, by their masters, and how murderously they drive their split stilettos into the bodies of the people! But they are the true sons of their fathers, who were used in the same way, forty years ago, to belie and crush the ABOLITIONISTS, but *failed!*

When off its guard, the American press itself—its pen mightier than Benedict Arnold's sword—lets out the whole secret. At a certain semi-public dinner, within the blessed memory of men not yet old—the champagne having ebbed low in the bottles—a distinguished journalist made a little speech. It was reported thus:

"There is no such thing in America as an independent press, unless it is out in the country towns. You are all slaves! You know it and I know it. There is not one of you that dares express an honest opinion. If you express it you know beforehand

---

* But one of the best-informed Englishmen ever in America—a man of very wide political, business, club, and press connections, on both sides of the Atlantic—tells me that, although this movement of subsidization is older in his country than in mine, the sharp, quick, Yankee press, is more completely under the thumb of the gold-trust than even its English organs. The most hopelessly rotten of all is probably our "Mugwump" journalism, which, with arms in angles and legs in strides, apes the stupid dignity of British affectation, as a long-tailed ulster to cover its bribes and frauds.

that it will never appear in print. I am paid $100 (per week) for keeping honest opinions out of the paper I am connected with. Others of you are paid similar salaries for doing similar things. If I should allow honest opinions to be printed in one issue of my paper, like Othello, before twenty-four hours, my occupation would be gone. The man who would be so foolish as to write honest opinions would be out on the street hunting for another job. The business of a New York journalist is to distort the truth, to lie outright, to pervert, to vilify, to fawn at the feet of mammon, and to sell his country and his race for his daily bread, or for what is about the same thing, his salary. You know this and I know it; and what foolery to be boasting of an independent press. We are the tools and vassals of rich men behind the scenes. We are jumping-jacks; they pull the string and we dance. Our time, our talents, our lives, our possibilities, are all the property of other men. We are intellectual prostitutes."*

The "subsidized press," however, is only one immoral offense of the epoch of the gold-bug. American "statesmanship"—God save it from annihilation—has sunk quite as low as American journalism. It is now perfectly evident that our two political parties which libel the holy names, "Republican" and "Democratic," are both little more than the decomposed spoils of London Jews and their New York twins of the English bank-system. Since the death of Lincoln, the Republican party has been completely in the toils of this combination—not wholly through knaves, it is true, but partly through the financial ignorance of tolerably honest men. For twenty-five years, the Democratic party has protested against the villainy of Lombard and Wall streets, as all the "Democratic platforms" show. Meanwhile, thousands of the most intelligent Republicans became Democrats on this account. But, as the plot thickened, a third-rate attorney was found in Buffalo, who happened, by the providence of folly and accident, to be at once a nominal "Democrat," an available candidate for the Presidency, and such a nightmare in political morality that he could be rolled, like Juggernaut in his car, on the remains of Thomas Jefferson, Andrew Jackson, and every other true leader of American Democracy. So a shout went up for Grover Cleveland, as the one "honest man" of his day. "Fame," said Napoleon, "that is noise." The noise once started, the fame increased, until "The Stuffed Prophet of Buffalo" had more throats in his service than ever "The veiled prophet of Khorassan." When he was pushed forward for

* On tracing up this extraordinary speech, I find that the moral substance of it was first popped off by John Swinton in 1883. It was "at a banquet of newspaper hacks," in New York, when called upon to speak to the toast, "The Independent Press." Mr. Swinton has always insisted, however, that his remarks were "clumsily reported," and that they contained no "infamous personal confessions." He meant, also, to make a clear distinction between scribblers, as the tools of others, and journalists as free to utter their own convictions. But Mr. Swinton, who has both "wrought and suffered" for truth, freedom and humanity, happens to be one of the readiest and wittiest speakers of his day, and his little extemporization was considered so funny that the journalistic brotherhood—often more picturesque than profound—"improved upon it," and put it into its present form, to which it has been attributed to half a dozen leading newspaper-men, among them Whitelaw Reid.

President, however, Democrats themselves exploded with derision at his claims, and the New York *Star*, referring to one feature of his career, said that "the Democratic Party" had "never yet been headed by a hangman." Whatever may have been the taste of such criticism, the Democratic "high executioner" has since hanged his party, and has nearly hanged his country.

In 1889, the Republicans resumed charge of the Federal Government, and, with them, as always, Wall Street commanded and scooped the Treasury. But, when the campaign of 1892 came, the great Anglo-American gold-plot, after a crusade of nineteen years against the silver dollar, had grown ripe. As a party—a series of platforms, a mass of voters—the Democrats stood solid in the way of the culmination of the villainy. But the English and Tory managers, who now controlled the wires of our American politics, saw that if a *Democrat* could be elected President, who would assume the role of Dictator, and would use the patronage of his office to bully and bribe his own party out of its promises and its record for a quarter of a century, then the American people might be utterly given over to their despoilers. *Hence Cleveland was preferred to Harrison*, though, between the two, the son of man was offered nothing but crucifixion.

To COVER THE GREAT GOLD-CONSPIRACY OF 1892, its foreign and domestic managers decreed the noisy agitation of two minor affairs— FEDERAL INTERFERENCE WITH ELECTIONS for the South, and for the North A CHANGE OF TARIFF—the tariff being a thing which the goldbugs themselves sneered at, as "a mere matter of schedules." Then the cooks and scullions of the press took their orders, as Democrats and Republicans, to deafen and beguile the people. What with the strictly English press, like the New York *Times* and the *Evening Post*, the boom-de-ay Jew press, like the *World*, the straight-Republican, straight-monopoly press, like the *Tribune*, and the bank-and-bullion Tory press in general, the work was done to the entire satisfaction of those who paid for it.

> "There on the throne to which the blind belief
> Of millions raised him, sat the Prophet-Chief,
> The great Mokanna.
> * * * * * *
> He raised his veil—the maid turned slowly round,
> Looked at him—shrieked—and sank upon the ground."*

It is a long time since the Democratic Party was a "maid"; but, after a look at Cleveland in 1893, she certainly gave one "shriek," and "sank upon the ground."

That our political campaign of the previous year was A PLOT, pure and simple, of the gold-contractionists against the American people, was soon proved by a million votes of those who saw through it, and by

---

* From Moore's "Lalla Rookh."

the words of their leaders who exposed it in advance. But the False-Prophet of the Tariff took his seat—on the American flag—and *then* the band of Rothschild, Sherman and Company, were quickly enough seen behind him. It was *they*, and *they alone*—this international syndicate of grabbers and wreckers—who, having sucked out the life-blood of all business for half a generation, by contracting the flow of money, *intentionally precipitated the panic of* 1893.

It is now pretty well known that, as early as the 12th of March—eight days after the inauguration of their President—the Bankers' Association issued to its members what has come to be known as

"THE PANIC BULLETIN."

"DEAR SIR : The interests of national bankers require immediate financial legislation by Congress. Silver, silver certificates and Treasury notes must be retired and the national bank notes, upon a gold basis, made the only money. This will require the authorization of from $500,000,000 to $1,000,000,000 of new bonds as a basis of circulation. You will at once retire one-third of your circulation and call in one-half of your loans. Be careful to make a money-stringency felt among your patrons, especially among influential business men. Advocate an extra session of Congress for the repeal of the purchase clause of the Sherman law, and act with the other banks of your city in securing a petition to Congress for its unconditional repeal, per accompanying form. Use personal influence with Congressmen, and particularly let your wishes be known to your Senators. The future life of national banks as fixed and safe investments depends upon immediate action, as there is an increasing sentiment in favor of government legal-tender notes and silver coinage."

Unlike the Hazard and Buell circulars, the "Panic Bulletin" may not, as yet, have been absolutely traced to its source. But, in this instance, such technical authentication is of no consequence, the whole programme having become a ghastly fact, which has *proved itself*. A resolute banker being asked about it recently by a friend, said he had no doubt it was genuine—for it was "about right"—though he had received so many circulars of the sort that he "could not be sure in regard to this special one." The manifesto merely laid out the well known "object-lesson" of breaking the business of the United States to stop the increase of silver money. This "object-lesson" was repeatedly threatened by the New York *Tribune* as long ago as 1877, and on December 24th of that year it said:

"Last week a long list of firms at Chicago was carefully filed away for future use by strong banks here. 'Why?' it was asked. 'Because this is a list of firms who support Bland's bill.' So spoke an old banker of note."

The Chicago *Inter-Ocean* of August 20th, 1893, said:

"Early in the winter a bank president, conversing with a Chicago man of business, said to him: 'Mr. Jones, we are going to make the West pay up this summer.' 'But why should you press your Western creditors?' asked Mr. Jones. The reply was: 'Well, we think it would make you a little more thoughtful about currency matters, and drive you from your foolish ideas about silver.'"

The comment of the *Inter-Ocean* was this:

"When the future historian tells the world of the great financial panic of 1893, he will say: 'In the winter and spring months of that year the New York bankers and financiers sowed the wind, and during the summer months reaped the whirlwind.' Colonel Ingersoll, early in the season of disturbance, properly called this 'a bankers' panic.' Nor are the New York bankers alone to blame. Those of Boston and Philadelphia come in for their share."

Reporting a conference between New York bankers and the United States Secretary of the Treasury, the *Sun* of April 27th, 1893, said:

"There is a determination also to show the miners of silver the evils of the Sherman law. * * * This work has been started by a number of bankers in the solid communities of the East. They are daily refusing credits to the South, Southwest and West."

On the 29th of April, the *Sun* added:

"The statement of Mr. Carlisle to the New York bankers makes it clear that while Mr. Cleveland works in Congress, the bankers will be expected to work, not in New York only, but throughout the country, doing their utmost to pinch business in the expectation of causing a money crisis that will affect Congress powerfully from every quarter."

The financial report of the Philadelphia *Press*, under date of September 22d, contained this frank confession:

"There are ominous rumors on the street that New York will again put the screws on the Senate. * * * *There is no question but that the banks of New York are still withholding money from merchants while possessing millions of idle cash, because of a tacit arrangement not to unloose it until the Senate votes for repeal.*"

The Philadelphia *Manufacturer* said to its readers on the 23d of September:

"The question has been, from the first, how far this panic was natural and unavoidable, and how far it was artificial and manufactured. * * * This 'scare' was evidently artificial in a large measure. It is moreover believed by many that it was deliberately planned to excite public distrust, to give excuse for the assembling of Congress, and to exert 'pressure' for the repeal of the Sherman act. It was to be an 'object lesson' to the country. * * * To endeavor to create, by manipulation and artifice, fresh financial distress, *is simply an attempt to commit a public crime, compared with which arson is trivial.* * * * One thing must be remarked in this connection: It will be a dire misfortune if the national banks of the country are betrayed into complicity with such of those in New York as are helping to concoct this scheme of public injury. Because, if they shall be—if the whole national-bank system is to be tarred with this infamous stick—how is it to be supposed they can be effectively supported when their time of trial comes, as it presently will? * * * Is it to be supposed that the mass of the people, if further convinced that the money-panic was artificial—in part or entirely a 'set-up job'—will rally in the banks' defense? Gentlemen, whoever you are, who propose to make distress wantonly, *you are playing with fire, and may perish in the flame of your own creating.*"

The banks, however, continued to "play" with their "fire"; and, by means of it, with the aid of the Sherman wing of the Republican party, a Democratic President made the final raid on American silver, and Shylock's scheme to plunder a world was at last consummated.

Is it to be supposed that GROVER CLEVELAND, who finally centered this whole conspiracy, is such an incarnation of "innocuous desuetude" that he has no understanding of his epoch, as he stands amid the ruins of it?

Senator Stewart, in a very significant speech of September 25th and 26th, 1893, entitled "Independence of the Co-ordinate Departments of the Government"—in which he exposed the panic-plot in great detail—said to the Senate:

"The matter of suspending the purchase of silver bullion, to cut off circulation and bring on a panic, are traced too near the Administration to avoid observation."

What is the use of delicacy with unfaithful public servants? To know Grover Cleveland it is only necessary to look at his Secretary of the Treasury. Here, doubt is done. This man has a *record*—one that stares him in the face, while it conducts him straight to realms below. On the 21st of February, 1878, John G. Carlisle said to the House of Representatives in Congress:

"I KNOW that the world's stock of the precious metals *is none too large, and I see no reason to apprehend that it will ever become so*. Mankind will be fortunate indeed, if the annual production of gold and silver coin shall keep pace with the annual increase of population, commerce and industry. According to my views of the subject, THE CONSPIRACY which seems to have been formed here and in Europe, to destroy by legislation and otherwise, from three-sevenths to one-half of the metallic money of the world IS THE MOST GIGANTIC CRIME OF THIS OR ANY OTHER AGE. The consummation of such a scheme would ultimately entail *more misery upon the human race than all the wars, pestilences and famines, that ever occurred in the history of the world*. The absolute and instantaneous destruction of half the entire movable property of the world, including houses, ships, railroads and all other appliances for carrying on commerce, while it would be felt more sensibly at the moment, would not produce anything like the prolonged distress and disorganization of society that must inevitably result from the permanent annihilation of one-half the metallic money of the world."

As long as currency must be redeemed in "specie" the words of John G. Carlisle, in 1878, will stand literally true. Nothing can change their ghastly import, unless the problem of money shall some day become an exact science, and all metals be relegated to the arts. In the present state of civilization—our debts being payable in coin, our paper-money and bank-ledger inflations resting on the same ultimate base—to deplete that base is to commit an all-inclusive crime, which entails every misfortune that can befall the human race. Under this system, Herod of Judea need never have commissioned his butcher-guard to "slaughter the innocents." A sufficient contraction of the currency would have starved the infants at the breast, and the fathers and mothers would have died with their babes. Better grip or cholera, better small-pox or yellow-fever, better all of them together, than the monetary results of the last quarter of a century.

JOHN G. CARLISLE knows all this, and HAS SAID IT. But on the 21st of November, 1893, he stood up at a banquet in New York, set at twenty dollars a plate by bankers and capitalists whose acts had brought three millions of human beings to idleness and hunger, and inverted the utterances of his departed honesty as unblushingly as the clown of a circus turns a handspring.

"It is enough [he exclaimed, amid the winks and leers around him] to say at present that we have already on hand a stock of silver, coined and uncoined, sufficient to meet all the probable requirements of the country for many years to come. * * * Gold is the only international money, and all trade-balances are settled in gold, or, which is the same thing, on a gold basis. It is useless for the advocates of a different system to insist that this ought not to be so. It is so, and we cannot change the fact. * * * The country has recently heard a great deal about bimetallism and a double standard. * * * For my part *I have never been able to understand what is meant by a double standard*, or double measure of value, and I have never found any one who could tell me."

If, by reason of established demand, two things of one kind are worth exactly one thing of another kind, we have a Secretary of the Treasury, it appears, who cannot understand how this "double-standard" can be a single "measure of value." In this condition of mind, at a banquet, he extinguishes his own biography, and the mathematics of money for thirty centuries. As a political attorney upside-down, he welcomes "war," advocates "pestilence," and eulogizes "famine." He invites, upon the heads of the American people, such "prolonged distress and disorganization of society" as could not be effected by "the absolute and instantaneous destruction of half the entire movable property of the world."

Not all American politicians, certainly, are floundering in such mire as this. But by long and patient iniquity, without regard to expense, our present brutalizing money-power appears to have left a majority of them with no principles not for sale. Among all "the signs of the times," what else is so nauseous or so dangerous?

CHAPTER XIV.

THE REMEDY.

THERE IS BUT ONE IMMEDIATE REMEDY for the demonetization of silver in this American republic, and that remedy is RE-MONETIZATION—the putting of silver back just where it was, when foreigners and traitors dared to interfere with it. But, while this is a point of dignity and patriotism, as well as of business, it will extend aid and encouragement to all true friends of American institutions in other lands. For instance, the great cleric of Dublin, Archbishop Walsh—the truest disciple of Christ, and the ablest man to-day, perhaps, in either the Protestant or the Catholic Church—has shown that while England is offering land and liberty to Ireland with one hand, she is slyly taking it back with the other, as the Irishman pays his dues to her in the rising value of gold.* Let us help to end all such British "statesmanship" of Jews in disguise.

American silver must be re-monetized at exactly the old ratio of 1861 and of 1872. WHY? Chiefly because every government bond we have out is *legally payable in silver coin at that ratio*. We must push the production of silver to the utmost extent, and give Shylock the flesh of his bond, without another drop of blood. Will he refuse it? The *bond*, Shylock, the *bond!* In the letter of it there is no *gold:* it is *coin*—the coin of 1861, and then the coin of 1872, when silver was at a premium over gold. You may have the *premium* now, dear Shylock, if you can find it. We will not stand about the *premium;* but the *silver* shall be put into your tigerpaw. Are you a foreigner, Shylock? And, as such will you resist HONEST MONEY? Will you try the game of England in Egypt—a Queen's army marching as a Jew's collecting agent? Then WAR, Shylock: it is better than peace, with your methods of destruction.

Again, the old American dollar must be wholly re-established, to condemn and destroy, forever, the precedents of recent days, by which the Government of the United States, through its chief executive officials, has been the most shameless violator of law that has come under its statutes.

Take one recent illustration. On the 14th of July, 1890, an act was passed "*directing the purchase of silver bullion, and the issue of Treasury notes thereon, and for other purposes.*" The language of the act was this:

"The Secretary of the Treasury is hereby directed to purchase, from time to time, silver bullion to the aggregate amount of four million five hundred thousand ounces, or so much thereof as may be offered in each month at the market price thereof, not exceeding one dollar for three hundred and seventy-one and twenty-five hundredths grains of pure silver, and to issue, in payment for such purchases of silver bullion, Treasury notes of the United States. * * *

"Such Treasury notes shall be a legal tender in payment of all debts, public and private, except where otherwise expressly stipulated in the contract. * * *

"The Secretary of the Treasury shall each month coin two million ounces of the silver bullion purchased under the provisions of this act into standard silver dollars, until the first day of July, eighteen hundred and ninety-one, and after that time he shall coin, of the silver bullion purchased under the provisions of this act, as much as may be necessary to provide for the redemption of the Treasury notes herein provided for. * * *

---

*"Bimetallism and Monometallism; what they are and how they bear upon the Irish Land Question." By the Most Rev. Dr. Walsh, Archbishop of Dublin.

"Upon demand of the holder of any of the Treasury notes herein provided for, the Secretary of the Treasury shall, under such regulations as he may prescribe, redeem such notes in gold or silver coin, at his discretion, it being the established policy of the United States to maintain the two metals on a parity with each other upon the present legal ratio, or such ratio as may be provided by law."

Except to some artful-dodger used in aid of kleptomania, how could anything be more definite than the purpose and the provisions of the Silver-Law of 1890? So much silver was to be purchased by the United States, at the market price, and coined into so many dollars of legal-tender money. Treasury notes were to be issued representing these silver dollars, the silver dollars having been expressly created to redeem the notes. But, that the silver-notes might be held equal to any other legal-tender money, the Secretary of the Treasury was empowered to pay them, on demand, in either gold or silver dollars, *at his discretion*, while the *sole purpose of the discretion* was to uphold "the established policy of the United States to maintain the two metals on a parity with each other upon the legal ratio." The Secretary of the Treasury was not instructed that one and one must make two in his accounts, nor was he instructed *how* to maintain the parity between gold and silver. The *mode* of maintaining such parity—and the *only mode*—is as fixed as the first problem of Euclid, and has been longer in vogue. There had never been an exception to it in the history of the world. To maintain the parity between gold and silver, a *debtor* simply pays his *creditors* in the coin he can best spare. As there is a certain total of coin in a country, and every debtor pays with that which he *has*, the parity between the gold and the silver is necessarily preserved, throughout the country that fixes the ratio. It is a pure certainty of mathematics. But, under the money-act of 1890, directing the United States Secretary of the Treasury to uphold the parity between gold and silver by paying out both for his country's debts, how did he execute the law? It was by DIRECTLY VIOLATING THE WHOLE PRINCIPLE, THE WHOLE METHOD OF PARITY, FROM THE FIRST USE OF GOLD AND SILVER AS MONEY IN THE TRANSACTIONS OF MANKIND. It was by turning the option of the *debtor* over to the *creditor*. It was by permitting Shylock, as the holder of government obligations, to dictate himself whether he would take gold or silver for them, *against a law of the United States* It was by entering into a plain, palpable CONSPIRACY with foreign and domestic enemies of the American people, to defeat exactly what he had been empowered and commanded to achieve. This CRIME is what was preposterously named the "policy"—the financial "policy"—of the Harrison Administration, and has been the still more open and brazen "policy" of Cleveland, officially sustained in several Messages to Congress. No wonder that General James G. Field, with a million votes of the South and West behind him, declared in July, 1893, that the Presidential Lawbreaker then in office "should be impeached."

But the worst count against the money-anarchs—the one united band of currency-contractionists, whether as demonetisers of silver or government-paper—and the best reason of all for thwarting their aims and correcting their misdeeds, is this: there is simply no doubt that they have contemplated, if not actually arranged, THE OVERTHROW OF FREE INSTITUTIONS IN AMERICA, if they can continue to rob us in no other way. As long ago as 1868, when, as bondholders, they had determined, *against the law*, to convert our whole national debt into immediate gold-value, these "extortioners," as John Sherman then called them, started a paper called "*The Imperialist*," to advocate, as its name implied, *imperial government as a sword for capital*.

"The paper was published at No. 87 Mercer street, New York. Its figure-head was an imperial crown, its motto, 'The Empire is Peace—Let us have Peace.' It was published by the Imperial Publishing Company, but was an anonymous sheet, no name of editor, proprietor or correspondent appearing on its pages. Among its advertisements was one of the banking firm of Morton, Bliss & Co. If rumor makes no mistake, Levi P. Morton was the senior member of the firm that gave its patronage to this traitorous sheet."*

"*The Imperialist*" introduced itself thus:

"Though *unannounced*, this journal is *not unexpected*. The platform of *The Imperialist* is revolutionary: its object is to prepare the American people for a revolution that is *as desirable as it is inevitable*.

* * * * * * *

"WE BELIEVE DEMOCRACY TO BE A FAILURE."

"We believe, in short, that Democracy means lawlessness, corruption, insecurity to person and property, robbery of the public creditors, and civil war; that the empire means law, order, security, public faith and peace.

"We believe that the national faith, if left in the keeping of the populace, will be sullied by the sure repudiation of the national debt, and that AN IMPERIAL GOVERNMENT CAN ALONE SECURE AND PROTECT THE RIGHTS OF NATIONAL CREDITORS.

"We believe that but A SMALL PERCENTAGE OF THE AMERICAN PEOPLE CAN BE CONSIDERED FIT, BY CHARACTER OR EDUCATION, FOR THE UNRESTRICTED EXERCISE OF SELF-GOVERNMENT."

"*The Imperialist*" first appeared in the early part of 1868. Grant became President in 1869. That great and true soldier, but a tyro in affairs of money, had pledged himself to the interests of Morton, Bliss & Co., with the other bondholders, who demanded, in return for their securities, money twice as costly to the people as the law and the contract called for. The sole purpose of "*The Imperialist*" was to double the bondholders' invest-

* The paper is well remembered by many people, including the writer, and various copies of it are still in existence; but the extract is taken from a little book, "Imperialism in America," by Mrs. Sarah E. V. Emery, of Lansing, Michigan—the authoress, also, of the celebrated brochure entitled "Seven Financial Conspiracies." A woman, writing two such tracts as these, takes laurels enough away from men. Perhaps "the mothers of the Republic" can yet awaken our intelligence and shame us into courage.—G. C.

ments and the people's taxes, or to *destroy the Nation.* The swindle accomplished, "*The Imperialist*" put out its candle—for the reason, as it stated, that "owing to the prejudice of the people and their love for THEIR FALSE IDOL, THE CONSTITUTION," the Imperialists could accomplish their designs better "through the Republican party."

We could afford to laugh, as we thought, at *The Imperialist.* But one fine day, ten years later, *The New York Tribune*—the leading organ of that Republican Party in which imperialism had merged—came out with the boastful revelation that

"The capital of the country is organized at last, and we shall see whether Congress will dare to fly in its face."

This vaunt was made on the 10th of January, 1878, and, the next day, the *Tribune* repeated it, thus:

"The machinery is now furnished by which, in any emergency, the financial corporations of the East can act together at a single day's notice, and with such power that *no act of Congress can overcome or resist their decision.*"

Precisely *how* "the capital of the country" was "organized at last," so that "Congress" was powerless "to fly in its face," is not yet clear in detail, though sufficiently evident, in general. Since the Hazard and Buell manifestoes got out, with the *Tribune's* premature explosion of would-be treason, the center of the unholy circle has become as select and secretive as its band of exemplars in "Cæsar's Column."* But, as surely as a George Washington, Thomas Jefferson, and Abraham Lincoln, framed, in the United States, "*a government of the people, by the people, and for the people,*" just so surely there is now a national and international attempt on foot to convert their work into an *absolute despotism of plutocrats, by plutocrats, and for plutocrats.* The worst recent step in this direction is the monstrous device of issuing government bonds over the dead body of assassinated silver money, that an increase of the national debt may be added to the burdens of industry, and that conspirators may grasp more sinews of power and oppression, while the poor shall have less means to resist them.

Though they have gone far with safety, let these conspirators beware. Their plot means ANARCHY; and the people are now asking this question :

"What difference is there in morals between the anarchists of poverty and the anarchists of wealth? The anarchists of poverty seek to divide among themselves and their followers the accumulations of others; and the anarchists of wealth seek to absorb the earnings of the masses by cunning and fraud." †

---

* The terrible and possibly prophetic novel by Ignatius Donnelly.
† *Senator W. M. Stewart in the "Arena" of August,* 1893.

The anarchist of poverty has been hanged at Chicago, and the anarchist of wealth may be hanged in New York and Boston. But the great Charter of this Republic will not be destroyed. It *is* our "IDOL"!
And now one further word on

FINANCIAL PANICS.

It is distinctly claimed in these pages that such panics are *wholly unnecessary*. They are nothing but the natural consequence of the English banking-system—wickedness robbing ignorance. How often we hear that "very little actual money is needed in business," because "the banks furnish ninety-five per cent of the facilities of commercial exchange." But here is just the trouble, just the danger and the ruin. Checks, drafts, clearing-house certificates—all such appliances—are indispensable to civilization. But, however we may settle accounts, if there is only *one* basic, redemptive gold-dollar to pay *ten* dollars in I-O-U's of banks—whether discounts on their books or bills they issue—then, the moment the gold dollar is actually needed to redeem more than *one-tenth* of its load of promises, that moment the dollar will *not go around*. The banks contract, and *must* contract, both the I-O-U's of their ledgers and their circulation: so the people can get no renewal of discounts, no money to pay their debts, and ten-dollars in *property* must be sold for anything it will bring, to get the one gold dollar—Shylock's dollar—the dollar of panics, with their "abomination of desolation."

This was our trouble in the summer of 1893. Let us see. According to the report of the Comptroller of the Currency, for 1890, there were then 3546 National Banks in the United States, having on deposit, subject to check, $1,596,000,000; other banks and trust-companies holding $1,014,000,000; and savings-banks, $1,524,000,000. The National banks then had on hand in gold, or Treasury-note equivalents, $290,500,000, and the other banks, all told, $185,254,000. The actual money out in the hands of the people was set down at $1,025,000,000. Thus the people had a working per-capita allowance of about fifteen dollars, which they were necessarily crowding to the wall, and the banks had more than *four billions* of credits balanced on *four hundred and seventy-five millions* of actual, redemptive currency. This structure was dangerous enough, at best. It required only a touch more of demand for gold at the base—a hair's breadth of contraction—to bring down the whole toppling mass. But the gold-conspirators WANTED A PANIC, and their bawling press freely threatened it. The Syndicate of Mammon called in gold—chiefly for export—and forthwith came the "crash." But then they turned round with the voices of fog-horns, and screamed: *"It is not we: it is silver—it is the Sherman bill!"* The idleness and poverty that have followed—the hunger and nakedness, the social disorganization, despair and death—all this is THEIR WORK. Behold the worst existing enemies of the human race!

The restoration to silver of its stolen property—the demand for it as full legal-tender money—will of course supplant just so much bank-inflation, just so many credit-bubbles, with the actual cash-dollars which the bubbles make the false and impossible promise to "pay." To the extent of the limited production of American silver, and the retention of it in our own country, such dollars will stop panics, even under our present money-system, while they will re-instate our great agricultural staples in foreign markets, and give back to us our natural and proper balance of trade. Best of all, such dollars will check the ravage of falling prices, which are now driving all production and trade into bankruptcy throughout the world. But, as already explained, all the gold and all the silver in existence—all "*specie*" whatsoever—can never furnish enough currency to do the work of MONEY. It is "a drop in the bucket." Treasury-notes—the glorious old "greenbacks" of "the War"—are the only money that can afford the deceived, defrauded and abused American people, sufficient and permanent relief. It has long been demonstrated, beyond question, that these notes, made legal-tender for all public and private dues, and limited in volume to the needs of exchanges and equities, are "as good as gold"; for, since 1879, they have been used as gold by banks to "redeem" *their* "money," and are so used to-day.

There is absolutely nothing new or strange in this proposition to constitute gold, silver, and United States treasury-notes, the equal and self-redeemable currency of the American people. It is "*the American idea*" as John Sherman might call it, if he should ever again indulge in the truth.

In regard to treasury-notes, Thomas Jefferson, in a letter to John W. Epps, under date of June 24th, 1813, said:

"And so the nation may continue to issue its bills as far as its wants require and the limits of its circulation will admit. * * * But this, the only resource which the Government could command with certainty, the States have unfortunately fooled away; nay, corruptly alienated to SWINDLERS AND SHAVERS, *under the cover of private banks.* Say, too, as an additional evil, that the disposal funds of individuals * * * have thus been withdrawn from improvement and useful enterprise, and employed in *the useless, usurious, and demoralizing practices of* BANK-DIRECTORS *and their* ACCOMPLICES."

Concerning loans for our second war with England, this same Thomas Jefferson wrote:*

"The question will be asked, and ought to be looked at, what is to be the recourse if loans cannot be obtained. There is but one—'*Carthago delenda est*': BANK PAPER MUST BE SUPPRESSED, AND THE CIRCULATING MEDIUM MUST BE RESTORED TO THE NATION

*Letter to Epps, September 11th, 1813.

TO WHOM IT BELONGS. It is the only fund on which they can rely for loans; it is the only recourse which can never fail them, and it is an abundant one for every necessary purpose. Treasury bills bottomed on taxes, bearing or not bearing interest, as may be found necessary, thrown into circulation, *will take the place of so much gold and silver,* which last, when crowded, will find an efflux into other countries, and thus keep the quantum of medium at its salutary level. *Let banks continue if they please, but let them discount for cash alone, or for Treasury-notes.*"

Thus, eighty years ago, THOMAS JEFFERSON—*the most elemental American yet given to his country*—laid down, in substance, the most pressing requirement of our own day. Clearly enough, if our industry and commerce are to have any safety, "bank-paper must be suppressed, and the circulating medium must be restored to the nation to whom it belongs." But this is not all. We have just seen that bank-credits to borrowers and depositors—all such discounts and trust-entries on bank-books—are just as much "inflations," and are just as dangerous, as bank-notes themselves, unless there is actual cash behind them for all emergencies. We have seen that, for this reason, confidence-banks of the British system must always "suspend specie payments," as often as really called upon to meet their full obligations. When our American banks of that system carry more than four billions of credits to the public on their books, and less than one seventh of the cash to pay them, how utterly ignorant, when not totally depraved, is the cry of "money enough—no more silver!" *Since the panic,* there has doubtless been money enough for the moment. For, after a man is dead, he can fly around as busily with one dollar in his pocket as with ten. But, if the business of the country is not to be the dead-man every five or ten years, *money* must displace and supersede both bank-ledger and bank-note inflations. Business must rest on *cash,* whoever may lend and whoever may borrow it. In the light of this palpable need, this easily-comprehended fact, is there any danger that the American people can ever have *too much silver?* All the gold and silver both, on the face of the earth, will soon be too little to make "HONEST MONEY" for OUR COUNTRY ALONE. The thimble-rig of the bankers and bullionists once out of the way, we shall *always* be obliged to enlarge our metallic money with government paper, if we are to be allowed *to keep at work and earn our bread.* As long, however, as gold and silver are "the basic money of the world," and as long as *we* are the chief producers of those metals, our duty to ourselves and to all other peoples, imperatively dictates that we should employ gold and silver to the best possible advantage, at home and abroad, *as far as it will go.*

PERFECT MONEY—"scientific money"—while quite possible to the future, is so far beyond the conception of to-day that even to indicate it is unnecessary. But the United States can at least adopt some approximation to the financial system of France, which insures industry and protects freedom, instead of following the English system to general impoverishment, and "a new form of slavery" for the masses of mankind. The French system has nothing of what Napoleon called "ideology" in it, but rests solely on experience and "the rule of thumb." The French, however, are so alert in their ways that they often reach a point better, by merely looking at it with the naked eye, than we heavy Saxons do with a Lick telescope or a Greenwich observatory.

The money of France is very largely metallic—gold and silver, both full legal tender to the extent of their issue, excepting a small amount of subsidiary silver. As a general thing the two metals are about equally divided in value, at the ratio of one grain of gold to fifteen and-a-half grains of silver. At present, the value of silver coin in circulation is said to be six hundred and fifty millions of dollars, the value of gold coin being somewhat more. As the territory of France is small and compact, and the population nearly stationary, her volume of money has become a pretty well known, and pretty well fixed, quantity. As she looks to it that her exports shall equal if not exceed her imports, and as she prefers trade with countries using gold and silver to gold alone, she *keeps* the money metals that have come to her from the store of ages—the largest proportion that any European country has accumulated. *But*, in case of war or other derangement of her affairs, her gold and silver flow out of her own domains. Then, as a Nation, as a Government, she turns to the BANK OF FRANCE, and makes *its paper-issues legal-tender money, to supply any deficiency of metallic currency that may take place.* Thus the volume of money—"the circulation of the life blood of the community," as the London *Times* once called it*—is kept flowing, and domestic industry is not strangulated. Financial panics are British and American institutions, and the French have no use for them.

But France is as careful not to overdo her money-volume, by paper or anything else, as she is not to underdo it. In time of need, the paper issues of the Bank of France are *irredeemable*—as much so as were the issues of the Bank of Venice. They make no atheistic promise to pay, "on demand," a quantity of metal that cannot be got, either from the stock of the nations or the bowels of the earth. But when the gold and silver, that some emergency has drained out of France, begins to return in settlement of her exports, *then* the Bank of France retires as many of her notes as the inflow of metal and the commands of the Government will permit. Thus "an elastic currency" of stable volume is achieved *by legal-tender paper*, while France, especially as a military nation that must always be ready for war, aims to have her full share of "the money of the world"— which she lends on occasion to the Bank of England.

A currency of gold and silver, with free-coinage, and with treasury-notes to supplement the inevitable deficiency of the "precious metals,"

* February 16th, 1849.

would be our natural American modification of French currency. Treasury-notes, like the similar issues of France through her Bank, would be absolute legal-tender for all private purposes, and redeemable in government-dues—revenues and taxes. It is now *settled in economics* that such money *would all stand equal*—absolutely equal—in any country emitting it *in properly limited volume*. This point, indeed, is the *only* one in connection with which capital as money needs protection—the protection of simple justice. Just money, whatever may be its mere fabric, must be *extended to*, and *limited by*, the need of its units to convey exchanges of property, while maintaining industries and equities. More than this, no people will ever ask; for man is both an upright and strangely patient being—ninety-five per cent of him, as shown by statistics. Shylock doubts it. Shylock fears to trust mankind. Why? Because Shylock himself is an *ingrain cheat*.

Precisely what volume of money should float in the United States, on THE PLAN OF THOMAS JEFFERSON here sketched, need not be dogmatically set down. If France—territorially a small, compact country—needs fifty dollars to a person in effective money, in order to avoid panics and crashes, it would certainly appear that this broad and sparsely-settled land should have *no less*. But this matter can only be settled, under our institutions, by THE WHOLE PEOPLE, through their servants, the law-makers of Congress. But these men must be *held responsible* for it as they have never been held responsible for anything before. As we have found that a bad currency is death to the people, and threatens death to the Republic, the politicians of our country may well take heed how such consequences shall affect *them*. BY LEGISLATION, and by legislation alone—the legislation of aristocrats in Europe and corruptionists in America—the old "automatic" system of money has been broken up. What was once the value of the precious metals, in proportion to the yield of nature and the custom of millenniums, has been completely changed, that one class of men—the class of Shylock—might plunder, denude and starve, the rest of the human race. BY LEGISLATION, the class of Shylock must be put into their proper place, and mankind be allowed to live. A department of the United States Treasury might be instituted, to fix honest money, under such safeguards and penalties, "even unto death," as would leave nothing to chance, venality, or serious mistake.

There are various methods by which the amount of money in a civilized country—all kinds of money—can be ascertained well enough. The amount in this country known for a start, there would be no difficulty in keeping track of it, and thus holding its volume in equilibrium. Exports of metallic money, in any considerable quantity, are known now, and all exports of it could be closely known without much trouble. On the outflow of coin, reserved "greenbacks" would simply be disbursed at the Treasury, for salaries, pensions, and public necessities, in quantity corresponding to the drain on gold and silver—exactly as the Bank of France, in like circumstances, acting as the fiscal agent of the French Government, pays out its blue-faced legal-tender. Thus the volume of domestic money would be kept up to the required use for it. But the United States, again like France, our exports naturally outvaluing our imports, could absolutely dictate and regulate the amount of *coin*, both gold and silver, best to be retained in our circulation. To reiterate, in conclusion, what has been fully explained and demonstrated, SILVER, or say the possessors of it prior to 1873, owned, through the laws and customs of the whole history of man, a certain estate, a certain property—*the legal-tender demand for it as money*—which was then stolen away. If by returning to silver its stolen goods, we the people of this great Republic can make that metal stand upright again, proudly equal to gold—*as we can do beyond all question*—then gold will be of no special account to us, even for importers and for corporations with creditors in England who have been 'promised gold-dividends on American securities.

There is no need of these evil days in which we live. They have been brought upon us by the avarice and chicanery of pure scoundrels. We have, at this moment, at least a hundred public men, any one of whom could dispel "hard times," set the industrious at work, and render the recurrence of a financial panic impossible forever, if only given the power to do it. There is NO DIFFICULTY in the case: 'tis merely a matter of HONESTY.

PUBLICATIONS FOR SALE BY THE AMERICAN BIMETALLIC LEAGUE.

Proceedings of the First National Silver Convention, November, 1889,	$0.20
Bimetallism and Monometallism. By Archbishop Walsh	.25
Speech of Hon. John P. Jones, United States Senate, 1893	.25
The Future of Silver. By Edward Suess,	.25
The Gold Standard. By Brooks Adams,	
Silver and the Science of Money. By Hon. Wm. M. Stewart,	.10
Jones' Chart and Tables, No. 5,	.10
Money and Prices. By Perry Prentiss,	.10
Per hundred,	5.00
True History of the Demonetization of Silver. Speech of Hon. Wm. M. Stewart, United States Senate, September, 1893,	.10
Money. Speech of Hon. John P. Jones, United States Senate, May, 1890,	.10
Facts about Silver (revised edition, 1894). Issued by American Bimetallic League. Single Copy,	.05
Per hundred,	5.00
Cause of Fall of Prices: The Change in the Measure and Not in the Goods. By Gen'l A. J. Warner,	.05
The Silver Question: How the Measure of Value is Changed. By Gen'l A. J. Warner,	.05
Prices on a Gold Basis. By Gen'l A. J. Warner,	.05
Important Financial Problems. Per hundred,	1.00
Single copy,	.02
The True Volume of Money at the Close of the War. Issued by the American Bimetallic League. Per hundred,	1.00
Single copy,	.02
Monetary Principles. Issued by the American Bimetallic League. Per hundred,	1.00
The True Volume of Money, January 1st, 1894. Issued by the American Bimetallic League. Per hundred,	1.00
Protection under the Gold Standard and under Bimetallism. By A. J. Warner,	.05
Both Sides of the Silver Question. By Jos. H. Monroe,	.25

www.ingramcontent.com/pod-product-compliance
Lightning Source LLC
Chambersburg PA
CBHW020105170426
43199CB00009B/398